gaudí

twentieth-century masters

gaudí

Lara Vinca Masini

Hamlyn
London   Sydney   Toronto   New York

twentieth-century masters
General editors: H. L. Jaffé and A. Busignani

© Copyright in the text Sadea/Sansoni, Florence 1969
© Copyright in the illustrations
colour: Raffaello Bencini e Liberto Perugi
black-and-white: arch. Aldo Loris Rossi
© Copyright this edition The Hamlyn Publishing Group Limited 1970
London · Sydney · Toronto · New York
Hamlyn House, Feltham, Middlesex, England
ISBN 0 600 33811 5

Colour lithography: Zincotipia Moderna, Florence
Printing and binding: Cox and Wyman Limited
London, Fakenham and Reading

Distributed in the United States of America by Crown Publishers Inc.

contents

List of colour illustrations

List of black-and-white illustrations

Ambiguity of language

Perhaps the greatest obstacle to a true understanding of the work of Antoni Gaudí lies in its fascinating and random ambiguity, the way it continually vacillates between a personal architectural vocabulary and conventional structure, even though his concept of a spatial theme is based in reality on recognisable structure rather than on any individual syntax.

This ambiguity, is, moreover, accentuated by the fact that the elements of his individual vocabulary are not always identifiable; indeed their origins are in turn rendered ambiguous and confused by something which intervenes before the syntax crystallises and which, like a distorting lens, imparts to them various colours and changes the emphasis of their form by different highlights. An unseen force plays freely with them – a fundamental biological force, drawn from an uncontrolled and uncontrollable ethnic inheritance of the kind which only Spain could offer with the background of a region like Catalonia, especially in Barcelona, that port open to the Mediterranean, the meeting-point of many races and cultures, 'a city of conquistadors and courtiers, of refinement, culture and luxury, the Athens of the troubadours'.[1]

All this is combined with his own personal sense of heightened, uninhibited fantasy, which makes him take up every stimulus from every source and develop it to extremes without caring if he sometimes borders on the superficial and amateur. (This characteristic may also be found in many of its aspects in the first explosive expression of, for example, Picasso or, sometimes, Miró, both of whom are from the same part of Spain, sharing the same Catalonian cultural environment and, in the case of Picasso, working at more or less the same time. Gaudí also shares the influence of the ethnic background of Catalonia where the most diverse peoples have mingled. The heritage of classical cultures for instance is not an influence which conditions or even tempers taste, but is only – and we see it in Gaudí as in Picasso – one of the various facets of the Catalan mind.

With Gaudí we come face to face with an extremely complex output which can be surveyed from diametrically opposed points of view and from different cultural and historical standpoints according to one's taste, education, or that particular need to acquire, absorb or transform that any culture feels when confronted with works of art that offer, as in Gaudí's case, such a vast range and such fantastic inventiveness.

Confrontation with Gaudí's realms of expression can indeed arouse varying emotions. These might take the form of the unreserved, irrational, and immediate admiration which is felt by the general, non-discriminating

Architecture as a spontaneous growth

1 R. Ford, *A Handbook for Travellers in Spain*, London, 1847, 2nd edition (quoted by J. J. Sweeney and J. L. Sert in *A.G.*, Stockholm, 1960; Milan, 1961).

1 Design for the restoration of the monastery of Poblet, executed with his schoolmates Eduardo Toda y Güell and José Ribera Sans, 1869–70

2 Desk for his own studio, 1878

3 Design for a shop-window for gloves, sent to the Paris Universal Exhibition, 1878

public and above all by his compatriots, for whom his work represents a sort of reincarnation ('*renaixenca*') because the most remarkable, magic and fabulous elements of Catalonia itself, epitomising elements singly or all at once, from the Late Gothic, Baroque, Mudéjar or from Catalan Modernism itself; or even from a dominant geological feature such as the mountain of Montserrat, as Casanelles has observed.[2] Or the reaction might take the form of complete incomprehension, turning to scorn. This last reaction falls in with those tendencies, which refute en masse every irrational or fantastic work of art in the name of a rigid extremist rationalism. Reaction against this rationalism has bred to a large extent the growing enthusiasm for the work of this great Catalan, the rehabilitation of Mannerism, the renewed study of Baroque and the discovery of the function of rejection by the avant-garde – seen in the rejection of Art Nouveau.

Gaudí has thus become the most powerful symbol of the reassertion of the Catalan nationality, expressed in the Federalist movement. This produced a whole new literary current promoting the rebirth of the Catalan 'language', which had been banned from the cities of Catalonia during the Castilian ascendancy; it fostered competitions for Catalan poets and medieval festivals of poetry, music and regional folklore like the Jocs Florals.[3] The Catalan independence movement was prevalently a movement to the right and, after 1876, following the defeat of the Carlists, was patronised by the Church. Gaudí's growing mystical exaltation led him to be adopted as the standard-bearer of fanatical and counter-Reformation Spanish Catholicism, which saw an embodiment of itself in his tumultuous expiatory Temple of the Sagrada Familia. The movement found in him a sympathiser and fanatical supporter and he willingly took up its cause. It might be said that this fanaticism bears witness to a lack of self-criticism and of clarity of judgement in his own work, which induced him to adopt the most diverse patterns of expression while adhering to fashionable or traditional forms, which he employed like a symbolic language to communicate some sort of message whereby he disguised – or often exalted in the most ingenuous fashion – the structural theme, which in reality was the true goal of his architectural aspiration.

Basically it was structure that interested him the most profoundly, in that it represented the only direct and unambiguous message of architecture. And it is the structural theme that is of special interest today because its foundations are a new experimental methodology following on from Gaudí's research at the time. Gaudí's experimentation (unlike today) was of a prevalently empirical character and, although his 'structural' theme was based on the application of the most recent discoveries in construction techniques and the latest notions of functionalism, he nevertheless used traditional materials like stone, iron, brick and wood, and, employing them still with the methods of the craftsman, sought to make the structure itself expressive, like a natural growth, striving at once to emulate and rival nature and the forces of creation. In this attitude he was part of the current wave of degenerate Romanticism, borne along by provincial Wagnerianism and the philosophy of Nietzsche, which, in the atmosphere of cultural eclecticism of the time, was evident in every work that was spontaneously applauded by the public as an expression of the 'collective spirit'.

Architecture as the demarcation of space

I have spoken of the 'direct and unambiguous' message of architecture à propos its function as the demarcation of space inasmuch as, while sharing the conclusions arrived at by present-day research, and particularly the observations of Dorfles,[4] Brandi[5] and Eco,[6] (for whom 'architecture chal-

2 In E. Casanelles' *Nueva Visión de Gaudí*, Barcelona, 1965.
3 The *Jocs Florals* were revivalist functions designed to exhume the artistic heritage as well as the poetic and medieval folklore heritage. They were revived in 1867.
4 G. Dorfles, *Il Divenire delle Arti*, Turin, 1959; *Simbolo, Communicazione, Consumo*, Turin, 1962.
5 C. Brandi, *Eliante o dell'Architettura*, Turin, 1956; *Segno e Immagine*, Milan, 1960; *Struttura e Architettura*, Turin, 1967.

lenges semiology . . . because works of architecture do not apparently *communicate* . . . but *function*' (Eco), and all architecture has a presence (Brandi) but does not communicate its function inasmuch as it *is* its own function.[7] But it does seem possible to me to find in the idea of the 'demarcation' of space in architecture (in the sense of a return to the absolute idea of space) its most direct communicative and communicable ingredient or the best key to unravelling its meaning.

The incredible assimilation in Gaudí's work has made it a mainspring for subsequent artistic movements in the contemporary artistic field. This is also due to his ability to adopt and transform the most disparate elements emerging from past cultures which creates (perhaps on a Freudian level) a sort of ancestral and protohistoric substratum not far removed from the refined artificial paradise of Huysmans' Orient (although without the turbid and sensual weighting which the name Huysmans implies).

It is this quality which caused him to be looked upon as one of the forerunners of Surrealism, and made Salvador Dali write in an article in *Minotaure* (1933), entitled *La beauté terrifiante et comestible de l'architecture Modern Style,* of the pleasure that Gaudí's art provoked in him when he penetrated 'grottoes through tender doors of calf's liver'.

It could be said that the zoomorphic references in Gaudí's work are always of a prehistoric type. One is led to think of defunct species of enormous antediluvian monsters, their flesh reduced to thick leathery strips of shrivelled and mummified hide, not at all 'tender', with flaking scales and horny crests, all luminous and pearly; of mountains transformed into dragons and seemingly alive; of the bone structures of hypnotised dinosaurs, in whose petrified veins black blood, thick as molten lead, stagnates—and it is as if when these monsters awake, everything will explode and catch fire like a volcano erupting. An observation made by W. Boeck emphasises the pre-organic character of Spanish artistic representation, and the dominant role played not only by, 'aspects of the animal world, but also the development from inorganic forms to living forms'.[8] It does not seem to me that one can find any reference here at all to the '*cadavre exquis*' of the Surrealists with its sickly and nauseous scent of pulpy flowers and putrefaction! Gaudí's recourse to primeval elements was rather a result of his need (characteristic of an isolated and closed personality such as his) to abandon himself like a child to dream of the fabulous and magical, to identify himself with these dreams and somehow to become one with his subject in a way which suggests a Pop rather than Surrealist approach to his work. His attitude towards his subject, however, is neither introverted nor sensual; he does not simply abandon himself to the forms of the unconscious or of dreams, nor does he evoke the subtle and disturbing shadows of subliminal worlds, as in the lyrical world of Surrealism. There remains the question of his relationship with 'magical realism', a relationship on which Alberto Sartoris[9] placed some emphasis in 1952. But this too is difficult and can easily be overstated.

Gaudí's ambiguity is perhaps more profound and unconscious; it takes place both on the level of solipsism and the vast unknowable more Nietzschean and Wagnerian—in the final analysis, perhaps, more localised and nineteenth-century, despite its powers of anticipation and foresight—than akin to Brueghel or Dali. Finally it is a condition which linked him to a 'national' movement in European culture and prevented him from recog-

Pre-organic character

4 Signed design drawing of the altar for a Neo-Gothic Chapel to be built at Alella, 1883

6 U. Eco, *Appunti per una semiologia delle communicazioni visive,* Milan, 1967; and also *Proposte per una semiologia dell'Architettura,* in 'Marcatre' nos. 34, 35, 36, Milan, December 1967.
  Other references: S. Bettini, *Critica Semantica e continuitá storica dell'Architettura,* in 'Zodiac', no. 2, Milan, 1958; S. Langer, *Sentimento e forma,* Milan, 1964; *Architettura come Mass-Medium,* Bari, 1967.
7 L. V. Masini, *La Cattedrale gotica come denotazione e individuazione di spazio,* in *Le grandi cattedrali gotiche,* Florence, 1968.
8 W. Boeck, *Meisterwerke von A.G.,* in the catalogue of the Gaudí exhibition in 1961 at the Society of Friends of Young Art at Baden-Baden.
9 A. Sartoris, *Gaudí poliforme,* in 'Numero', 1952, vol. IV no. 3; and also: *Polimorfismo de Gaudí,* in 'Papeles de son armadans', Vol. XV, no. XLV, December 1959.

nising on a conscious level the real revolutionary undercurrents which were to be brought to the surface by the artistic avant-garde of the twentieth century and by the struggles for democratic liberty which the nineteenth-century wars and revolutions of national independence, smothered in a blanket of 'patriotic' ideals, had not succeeded in furthering. These under-currents flowed in Gaudí's mind too but they were not necessarily always evident or even conscious. They are the clue which enables us to recognise him as forerunner of the avant-garde movements, from Art Nouveau to Expressionism, Cubism, Dadaism and abstract art in the Mudéjar orientalism of his first works, the organic forms of the wall of Casa Milá, the bewitched warrior-chimney stacks on the roof and the billowing walls of the School of the Sagrada Familia, in the magic collages of the ceramic tiles on the serpentine bench which encircles the elevated area of square in the children's garden in the Parc Güell and in the delicate, smoky colour of the façade of the Casa Battló with its clear crest of azure green.

These are all engaging hypotheses and revelations and they are also essentially true in themselves, but they are all retrospective notions that were not always present at the level of Gaudí's consciousness or artistic intentions. Nevertheless at the time the power of Gaudí's imagination was such that every means of expression that he adopted was inexorably transformed and made live and vibrant, constituting a revolution and a prophetic artistic break-through.

Space – an unambiguous message

This study should perhaps be based more precisely on Gaudí's ideas of structure, which are less ambiguous even if they are not always as obvious as other more important aspects of his work; thus it was necessary to determine the vocabulary of his styles in order to find the true and direct message of his architecture, which is essentially of a spatial character.

Space expanding outwards

The sense of space which Gaudí wanted to achieve was primarily that of space expanding outwards, with the feeling of confined forces striving to explode.

5 Design for the lamps for the Muralla del Mar at Barcelona, 1880

Gothic space, for example, had a radial expansion based on elastic tensions, but this had been a unilateral expansion along fixed and calculated lines leading strictly in one direction, so that, particularly on the inside of a building, a closed network was formed which was constantly tightening its mesh and felt constricted despite its inflated scale which, for the very reason that it was out of proportion with the size of man, only seemed to heighten the sensation of perplexity and oppression. Baroque space, too, had been a dynamic movement, a negation of the confined and rigid spatial concepts of Classical and Renaissance architecture—at least that had been the intention when this style first developed; it was a taut, dynamic concept of space, but one which was designed, calculated and limited—the impending explosion was programmed and controlled.

The hyperbolic curve which typifies Gaudí's exploration of space is indeed an outgoing curve, projecting itself physically from the floor into space. It bears no relation to the sinuous and vital but non-organic, linear or spatial curve of Art Nouveau, although one cannot dismiss Gaudí's relationship with Catalan modernism and it should not be forgotten that he was working during the time of the outbreak of 'Modernism' and that Catalonia at this time saw not only the work of Gaudí, but also that of Domerech i Montaner, Martorell, Vilaseca, Berenguer, Cadalfaclo, Granell and Rubio i Bellver.[10] Gaudí's curve varies continually in direction, guided by natural expansion, by organic growth and by a sort of internal charge of dynamite ready to make it explode in all directions and destroy its identity. The curve of a Borromini, for example, is dynamic and leaping, but calculated; it opens and closes upon itself with an entwining movement and contains within itself an interplay of forces which are highly elastic and allow it to dart and

10 O. Bohigas, *L'Architettura modernista. Gaudí e il movimento catalano,* Turin, 1969.

bound but which never let it go. Gaudí's curve grows, struggling and contorting itself like a natural element, sometimes in a straight line, then shattering and coming together again. It conquers and dominates space again and again, exalting itself in its growth, expanding and contracting. And the moment arrives when Gaudí's fantasy begins to summon up monsters, and obeying some subconscious need to become one with his creation (and in this phase we can see a Freudian influence), it hurls formless matter against the structure, making it explode and settle back on itself. Then it lies dormant, a monstrous beast in its fluorescent bed of volcanic ash, dazzled by the pyrotechnic games of the enchanted castles rising from the embers.

But at the root of this violence and in spite of it there lies the seriousness and severity of Gaudí the constructor and designer.

In reality every work is a struggle in which he is putting himself and his ideas to the test until he finds what he wants to create, drawing inspiration from the mainstreams of inventiveness the world over.

For example we can see, particularly in the Sagrada Familia, his rapport with Gothic, which remains the touchstone of his work, for he succeeded where other Gothic Revivalists failed. Their buildings rose under the stimulus of half-literary formulae, justified by particular social and political conditions, whereas Gaudí re-created, through his fervour and visionary religious fanaticism, the same spiritual and psychological need which had made the blossoming of Gothic space possible in the Middle Ages.

Gaudí was not a 'revivalist' in the common sense of the term; in fact, he challenged the concepts of Gothic and its vital constituent elements. He re-examined its structural context and put forward different solutions; he broke down the rationalistic rigours of the tripartite structure (ogive, flying buttress, buttress) on which the thrusts are balanced, and re-employed them in the hyperbolic curve which transformed them into a spatial element, a hyperbolic paraboloid, in such a way as to cancel out every other interposed element which divides or balances the thrusts, retarding the thrust and the upwards impulse. This he achieved by means of columns 'which are angled to absorb the necessary loads, doing away with buttresses and flying buttresses and absorbing the forces in a new static structure unburdened by supplementary loads'.[11]

6 Design for a fountain for the Plaza de Cataluña, Barcelona, 1870

7 Design for the entrance to a cemetery, 1870

The efforts he made to regain from cultural traditions, albeit from an eclectic culture, those elements which constitute the basic structure of his architecture (seen most noticeably in the crypt of the Chapel of the Colonia Güell at Santa Coloma de Cervelló, and in his plan for roofing on the Sagrada Familia) were rewarded in his discovery of the infinite series of possibilities inherent in the identification of the central structural element, namely the hyperbolic curve, customary in Catalan vaulting and often found elsewhere in its architecture. Gaudí took this element and recreated it from its original state as an elementary part of popular language into something with an individual character which he extended to all its possible applications until it became a means of expression.

Identification of the means of expression

One of the guiding lines to a study of Gaudí's development may be found by following the evolution of this basic element, the hyperbolic curve, in its transformation from a linear element to its use in planes with hyperbolical and dynamic spatial forms and in variations of it in complex plastic structures such as paraboloids, hyperboloids and helicoids. We will start with an examination of the parabolic curve which had already appeared in the small lateral cupolas of parabolic section in his project for a fountain in the Plaza de Cataluña at Barcelona (1870); and the monumental arch proposed for the entrance of a cemetery done as an academic exercise (1870); (R. Pane

The Odyssey of a form

Fig. 6
Fig. 7

11 J. Perucho-L. Pomés, *Una arquitectura de anticipación,* Barcelona, 1967.
12 R. Pane, *A.G.,* Milan, 1964.
13 C. Martinell, *A.G.,* Barcelona, 1967.

also speaks in his study of Gaudí's early works of the acroteria 'connected in a curve' which 'take their cue from two opposed cones, that is from the embryo form of the hyperboloid'.[12] It had appeared too in the balustrade of the monument at Aribau and in the park of the Ciudadela at Barcelona (1876–77) in which the greater proportion of his biographers see evidence of his collaboration with the engineer Fontsere, when he was still a student. More recent studies, particularly that of Martinell,[13] refute this attribution, as well as that of his collaboration with F. de P. del Villar at the *camarín* of the Virgin of Montserrat.

8 Design for a social centre for the La Obrera Mataronense co-operative, 1878–82

9 Design for a patio for a provincial government, 1870

10 Design for the head office of the Franciscan Mission at Tangiers, 1892–3

The theme of the hyperbolic curve was carried further in the roof of an industrial pavilion for the co-operative, 'La Obrera Mataronense' (1878–82) which bears a reference to Viollet-le-Duc, one of Gaudí's guiding lights. It contains in the great gate in brick and ceramic for the Finca Güell (1883–85), the vast arches of the lodge of the same building and its detail; the doorways and ogives of the windows of the Palacio Güell (1885–89); and the radial openings of the Archbishop's Palace at Astorga (1887–92). One of the clearest examples of the application of the hyperbolic curve is that which runs right through the convent of the Theresians (1889–94), where it is used as a subtle element of spatial division. Finally, in the project for a Franciscan monastery at Tangiers (1892–93), this element reached the summit of its development, achieving a spatial synthesis which unites the abstract metaphysical motifs of Gothic spatial theory with all the arabesque fantasy of the Orient in a fairytale setting. The spires of the Tangiers project still have a conical rather than parabolic profile but they presage, with their reciprocating interconnections, the spires of the Sagrada Familia. In the leaning columns of the crypt of the chapel of Sta Coloma de Cervelló, in the arches and tree columns of the viaducts of the Parc Güell, in all the masking of the windows and doors and the crested roof of Casa Battló, in the curved wall and complex conformations of the roof of the little school near the Sagrada Familia, in the façade of Casa Milá and finally in the plastic complexities of the roof walks and the tapered parabolas of the spires of the Sagrada Familia, the odyssey of a form was made complete and given its fullest range of expression.

A forward-looking architecture

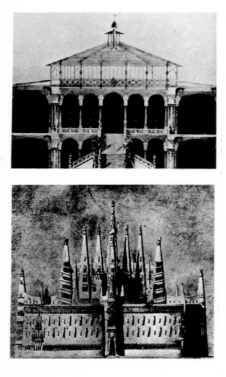

The perseverance, persistence and obstinacy with which Gaudí pursued, amplified, perfected and modified a form, right throughout the course of his life, constitutes a notable testimony to the depth of his research, which therefore emerges as more coherent and deliberate than is suggested by the far-fetched creations, mirages and fantasies to which he abandoned himself, or by the extravagancies and indulgences in popular whim which make up the other, better known and in many ways more fascinating aspect of Gaudí's architecture. His work is characterised too by a continuous and stimulating review and revision of the styles of the past, into which he injected advances in constructional techniques and other technological discoveries. This conscious acceptance of past styles was to save civilisation from the progressive alienation and aridity of the mechanistic technology which was already dominating the world and which before him Ruskin, Morris and Van de Velde had tried, at the risk of over-involvement, to channel and guide. This was also the intention of Art Nouveau to try to present art as the guiding mentor, the creator of models for industrial production, and succeeded only in creating the concept of the 'de luxe' object which was appropriated and vaunted by the very neo-capitalist society against which the movement had been directed. It might be said that this was the same danger of engulfment by the system to which in our age all movements of revolutionary intent are exposed, for the destructive power of the system is very great. An example of this was the fate of rationalist architecture in Italy, which was adopted as the architecture of the Fascist régime (and completely nullified). This too was to some extent the fate of Expressionism in Hitler's Germany. It is against the destructiveness of the system that today the young generation from hippies to Marcusians and the university movements are hurling their challenge. (But in this instance the dynamic impulse of 'protest' remains

valid, even in protest against itself. This is perhaps one of the most authentic and substantial achievements of our time.)

In the work of Gaudí this struggle in ideological terms takes on almost reactionary qualities. It should not be forgotten that, except when in his youth he showed a certain interest in socialist ideas, belonging to the 'Societat de la Obrera Mataronense' and working on projects for workers' housing, factories and community centres, he always worked for the upper classes and for wealthy patrons, even though they may have been enlightened ones. On the other hand the fate of the architect is in the hands of his employer, and without an Eusebio Güell we would probably not have had as important an achievement as that group of Gaudí's work, certainly not in today's society, even in Spain in Gaudí's day. The fact that he worked under the eye of a patron provides further proof of the forcefulness of his personality and the extraordinary strength of his creative invention, for his architecture was decidedly open and immediate, as Perucho[14] defines it, a forward-looking architecture. The essential difference, however, between Gaudí's work and that of the 'Modernists' has been nicely identified by Zeri: 'Gaudí . . . refutes the idea of a discourse based upon the juxtaposition of motifs out of their context . . . he aims at a free but organic architectural composition, at a polyhedral mass, twisted this way and that to vitalise every fibre and liberate its every dynamic potentiality, yet fluent and united like a hollow terracotta form . . . Gaudí respects the past because he finds a spiritual adventure in it, a burst of fantasy which scorns compromise and meanness and hurls abuse at Classicism.'[15]

Architecture as 'liveable' space

Gaudí's attempt to master a form of expression which could transform the cramped and inadequate living space of modern man and the unplanned, dehumanised and formless mass of the modern city can be put side by side with all the subsequent efforts to produce a 'liveable' space for man. Frank Lloyd Wright and other modern architects tried to evolve a plan for existence, such men as Louis Kahn, Kinsler and Michelucci. One parallel which cannot be made is with Le Corbusier, whose church at Ronchamp has been construed as an organic and 'irrationalist' (Pevsner)[16] expression of Corbusier's ideas (and has been wrongly compared with some of Gaudí's experiments).

The ideas which Corbusier presents at Ronchamp constitute a precise and highly rationalistic example of architectural methodology. The building's purpose is to project his theories through its various constituent parts. It is 'an act of intelligence and sensitivity on the part of a man who, when he considers reality, is able to put himself under the spell of any slogan – even his own – because he is free to interpret it according to its concrete needs'.[17]

Nor can Gaudí's work be associated with the subsequent avant-garde movements which sought to regain man's freedom not by means of a return to the origins of the world and its inorganic state, charged with uncontrolled and primeval ferments and impulses, but rather if at all by gathering together and understanding in an intellectual and civilised way the historical and cultural contingencies of existence. Malevich's *White Painting,* for example, is the absolute zero, the blank white page of the man who has 'read all the books' and has found the sum of all colours is white.

Gaudí, for his part, is saturated in colours, dazzled by colour in all its physical, analogical, symbolic and cultural manifestations. An unquiet spirit, unfulfilled, ever more closed and uncommunicative, and in the final analysis, a misfit, in reality fearful of living if not cushioned from poverty, he took refuge in colour, which stunned him as it does a child. Colour was to be the root of his functionalism and his decorativism; it was to be the means of his constant search for dynamism; colours, ever more sombre,

14 Perucho-L. Pomés, *Op. Cit.*
15 B. Zevi, introduction to O. Bohigas, *Op. Cit.*
16 N. Pevsner, *Pioneers of Modern Architecture,* New York, 1949.
17 E. Rogers, *Il metodo di Le Corbusier e la forma della Cappella di Ronchamp,* in 'Casabella-continuità', no. 207, Milan, 1955; now in *Esperienza dell'Architettura,* Turin, 1958.

were to represent his refuge in an involved and even troubled religious mysticism. It is colour which contains the symbolism with which he charged the already overburdened Nativity figures of the portal of the Sagrada Familia.

Early works

Gaudí's early works display a worldly and to some extent publicity-seeking attitude which is in line with his use of ostentatious formulae designed to flatter the intellectually snobbish tastes of the intelligentsia of Barcelona, which showed a paternalistic desire to encourage movements of a vaguely socialistic character, especially if such movements could be absorbed into the more general nationalist movements. This movement prompted the young Gaudí to join the 'Centre Excursionista' which organised collective excursions of young intellectuals and nationalists to the places sacred to the 'racial' self-assertion of Catalonia, from Montserrat to Majorca, Pic de la Maladeta, Tolosa and Carcassonne. It is interesting to record an episode which must have excited Gaudí's enthusiasm as a novice. His visit to Carcassonne coincided with the time when Viollet-le-Duc was about to begin his restoration work there, and Gaudí was mistaken for Viollet-le-Duc by one of the inhabitants when intent on inspecting the ancient walls of the town. This gives some indication of how clearly defined and how well developed his interests already were.

13 Casa Vicens, Barcelona, 1878–80 Exterior in its original state

14 Casa Vicens, Barcelona Detail of the open veranda in its original state

It should be noted that he was at the time studying Viollet-le-Duc's work very closely; there exists a copy of the *Dictionnaire*,[18] which he borrowed from a friend, with the margins crammed with notes in his hand.

While still a student, Gaudí had become associated with the organisers of the Catalan co-operative movement called the '*Societat Obrera Mataron-ense*' for which, shortly after qualifying as an architect, he made designs for a number of urban projects from factories and a complex of buildings for the working class to a community centre. The only buildings actually carried through were a small kiosk and an engine-house at Mataro near Barcelona. To support the engine-house roof he employed a succession of wooden parabolic arches, following a method found in ancient Catalan tradition. (In this connection Roberto Pane cites, by way of a comparative example, the naves of the *drassana* at Barcelona, the novices' dormitory at the monastery of San Creus). But it was based, above all, on ancient French models which were well-known at the time, not only through Viollet-le-Duc's *Dictionnaire* but also through the publications of Rondelet and others.[19]

While his youthful projects, from the monumental entrance to a cemetery and the lamp standards for the Plaza Real in Barcelona to, somewhat later (1880), his illumination of the Muralla del Mar at Barcelona and of the Paseo Nacional in Barcelloneta, indicate a constant search for a form of expression, it is in his first important structures – Casa Vicens, Barcelona (1878–80), the Finca Güell at Las Corts de Sarria near Barcelona (1883–85), the villa El Capricho at Comillas near Santander (1883–85) that we find the first full assertion and affirmation of a definite cultural attitude and position, although this is not without traces of his personal ambition and to some extent this work is imposing for the purpose of professional success. However, one cannot really speak of him, as has happened (Cirlot[20] and Pevsner[21]), as a 'precursor of the *modern style*, fourteen years before Horta'. Horta consciously initiated a 'new style' and put forward a revolutionary social and cultural ideology in his Maison du Peuple at Brussels. Gaudí's intention in Casa Vicens, the Finca Güell and El Capricho was only to 'affirm a new trend in taste', drawing on the rich coloration of Mudéjar art (the art of the Arab community in Spain, converted to Christianity after the Aragonese conquest of Spain in 1492) which had previously been exposed to the Catalan public.

18 E. Viollet-le-Duc, *Dictionnaire raisonné de l'architecture française du XIème au XVIème siècle,* Paris, 1854–69.
19 R. Pane, *Op. Cit.*
20 E. Cirlot, *El arte de* G., Barcelona, 1950.
21 N. Pevsner, *Op. Cit.*

His use of stone and brick as facing materials, his extensive use of majolica, his emphasis on projecting terracotta structures in a scaled progression and his frequent employment of wrought iron (for which Catalonia has a great tradition dating from the Middle Ages and which enjoyed renewed importance at this time)—all these indicate that Gaudí was distinctly a revivalist, an element which was to survive even his most positive steps towards an independent architectural style. Examples of this tendency are to be found in the Casa Vicens in the beautiful tiled fountain forming a parabolic arch (later destroyed to make way for a lodging-house), in the building's angular elements and in the palm leaf motif executed in the form of a hyperboloid and used in the iron railings and the terminal points of the roof. (This was to prove one of the motifs anticipatory of Art Nouveau, being featured on the cover of a book by Mackmurdo, and was to become one of the most characteristic naturalistic elements of Gaudí's own style.) At the villa El Capricho, this search for autonomy manifested itself in the free distribution of internal spaces and the lighting of the interior involved the recognition of the role of light in architecture. At the Finca Güell the characteristic features were the forms born of fantasy and their employment in a plastic structure. It should not, however, be forgotten that this was the time of the experiments of the Chicago school, and, as an example of innovation in structure, John Roebling's Brooklyn Suspension Bridge in New York was built at about this time, in 1875.

Fig. 15

Fig. 12

Gaudí built Casa Vicens (1878–80) for a humble brick manufacturer who was practically ruined by the expense involved but who later was able to profit amply from the subsequent popularity of ceramic tiles for house façades which stemmed from its successful use on his own house. It was later (1925) enlarged and extensively remodelled by the architect, J. Baptista de Serra Martinez, who was appointed with Gaudí's consent, although at the time Gaudí was fully immersed in the problems posed by his Sagrada Familia and had no longer any interest in the fate of his earliest work. It is therefore difficult today to reconstruct its original appearance. The interior of Casa Vicens follows a fairly traditional plan and is dominated by decorative motifs of an eclectic and often heavy nature. However, the Moorish motif on the ceiling of the *fumoir*, decorated with stalactite forms, is quite interesting and shows a certain freshness of interpretation. It is built up around the chandelier, lighting the room in a way which combines natural light-sources with artificial ones.

The villa El Capricho (1883–85) at Comillas is perhaps more characteristic of Gaudí, not only in the free distribution of internal space but also in the more deliberate light effects of the narrow apertures and rounded shapes of the exterior and the rhythmic sunflower motif in high relief on the ceramic tiles which cover the whole building, providing multiple viewpoints. It is also more representative in its new interpretation of the potential of light in the open relationship between interior and exterior, and shows his attention to the function of every meticulous decorative detail (particularly on the basis of light elements and their rhythm). But Gaudí never went to Comillas, which is situated near the coast of the Bay of Biscay, and the villa was built entirely according to instructions he gave in his absence. This contrasts very much with Gaudí's more usual continual attendance on site. It seems likely that he sent a sizeable plaster model, complete in every detail, to Comillas. The plan of the villa moves freely from level to level around a large conservatory. This scheme permits many openings and passages and makes of this building, which nevertheless possesses elements of deliberate culturalism and exhibitionism, a remarkable plastic form which culminates in the round tower (or *mirador*) with its faceted polygonal cupola hanging in the void above the plant like embroidery of an iron balustrade.

Roberto Pane published pictures of a wall recess in brick and white tiles and a stairway, both in the garden. J. F. Ráfols, who alone recalls so many lost works by Gaudí, mentions neither these latter details nor indeed the villa itself. The brick and white ceramic recess, set into an embankment in

15 Casa Vicens, Barcelona Garden fountain with parabolic arch, now demolished

16 Villa el Capricho, Comillas, 1883–85. Alcove in brick and white ceramics in the garden

17 Finca Güell, Las Corts
de Sarria, Barcelona, 1883–7
Detail of the wall decoration

18 Finca Güell, Las Corts
de Sarria, Barcelona. Gate pillar

the garden, has projecting pilasters at each end, a step-like effect being achieved by means of superimposed tiles. This was perhaps the first idea from which evolved the rustic vases surmounting a number of 'grotesque'-style pilasters in a viaduct in the Parc Güell. But it does also suggest an important affinity with certain 'projecting' motifs characteristic of the early work of Frank Lloyd Wright (and additionally with the 'mushroom' columns in the same Parc Güell and in Santa Coloma de Cervelló).

The two pavilions at the Finca Güell also show a Mudéjar inspiration. These were meant to stand on the boundary of the Güell estate, and the Finon was Gaudí's first job for Eusebio Güell, which he carried out between 1883 and 1887 at Las Corts de Sarria, then in open country but now Avenida de Pedralbes and on the campus of the new University of Barcelona.

These two pavilions display a fairy-tale element in their bright, vivid colours and their luminous preciosity, in the plastic forms of the great thrusting chimney of the lodge and the lantern on the dome of the house, in the enormous winged dragon in traceried and wrought iron forming the Fig. 19 entrance gate. The wall decoration contains an arabesque motif in its inter- Fig. 17 secting semi-circular shapes. These features display some of the characteristics which were to become peculiar to Gaudí's world. These characteristics were the generous employment of ceramic tiles to provide chromatic links

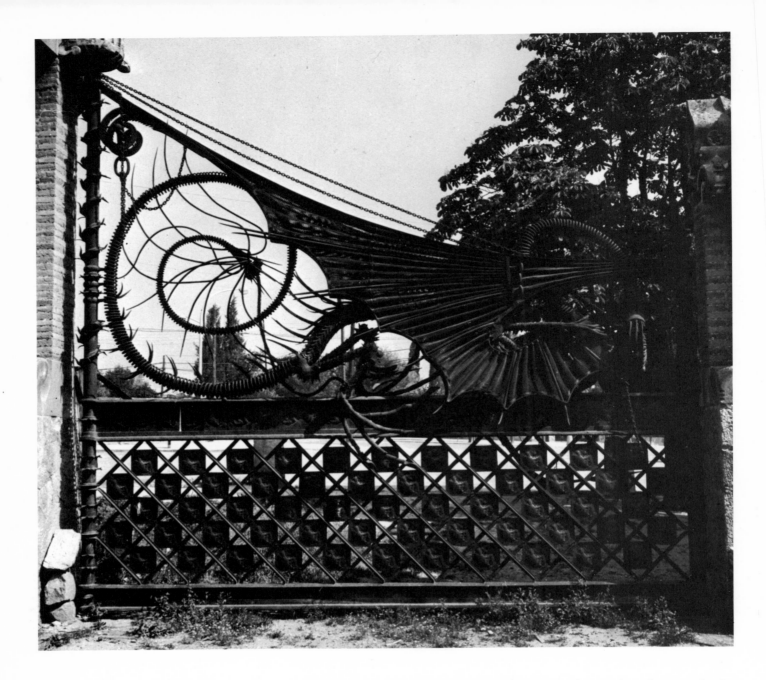

and a rhythmic play of light as a non-figurative decorative element (as in the Casa Vicens and the villa El Capricho) the free plastic composition of the forms and the architectural virtuosity of the roof, with flat terraces, domes, cupolas, and lanterns, all by bold step-forms in brick. This latter feature crowns the upper part of the Palacio Güell, the dominant roof structure of the Casa Battló and the resplendent and impressive roof of Casa Milá. The distribution of space inside was also organically defined. The stables develop along a sequence of parallel parabolic arches standing on corbels and spaced with barrel vaulting. The house, leading straight on from the stables, is in the shape of a flat dome surmounted by open work walls as in a lighthouse. Above this blossoms the jewelled cone of the short cupola with its radiating petals.

The magic is maintained in the fanciful use of wrought iron at the summit of the jewelled pilaster at the entrance and above all in the enchanted iron dragon, the product rather of a magical underlying alchemy, a 'mannered' medieval inspiration, than of the disturbed fantasy of a 'surrealist' mind. The dragon image is merely suggested and is only clearly defined in the head, which recalls late Gothic monsters and the innumerable representations of St George and the dragon in wood-engravings after the fifteenth century, which might be said to have been the first art for the masses.

22 J. F. Rafóls, *Op. Cit.*

19 Finca Güell, Las Corts de Sarria, Barcelona, Iron gate with zoomorphic shape

The Finca Güell also possessed a brick staircase, now destroyed, and a brick and ceramic gate which is now completely travestied by a heavy-handed restoration which makes it look Pharaonic. Its original appearance can only be seen in an illustration published by Ráfols.[22] Based on a parabolic arch and relying entirely on the natural appearance of its unadorned materials, it stood in the boundary wall. Now isolated, it has lost most of its character.

Fig. 22
Fig. 23

With the Palacio Güell (1885–89), which was begun two years before the Finca Güell, Gaudí had reached a stage near the summit of his architectural autonomy.

Although it has been said that this building shows a return to Venetian Gothic, it is more pertinent to speak of Moorish elements, which themselves can be found in Venetian architecture, which permeate the building as a whole. In fact various stylistic features are freely adopted here, as much from deliberate choice as from random personal predilection. The Palacio was no more the product of a revivalist taste than it was an impulsion to take the elements of different architectural styles into review and combine the embroidery of Moorish architecture and through this the airy Venetian architecture with the colourful picturesque flexibility of the Spanish house, opening on to the patio with its play of elements in the filtered light and its interrelationship between the interior and the exterior—jealously shrouding its inner secret, at the same time from the outside vaunting its hidden treasure, veiled provocatively like the eyes of a beautiful Scheherezade, only briefly glimpsed.

The façade of the Palacio Güell is based on the necessity of its having a clearly defined relationship with the street to which it is linked by two great

Palacio Güell

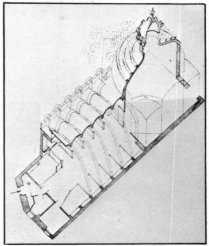

20 Sectional view of the stables and house of the Finca Güell, Las Corts de Sarria, Barcelona

21–23 Finca Güell. Detail of the exterior; brick and ceramic staircase, now demolished; gate in brick and ceramics, now extensively remodelled, in its original state

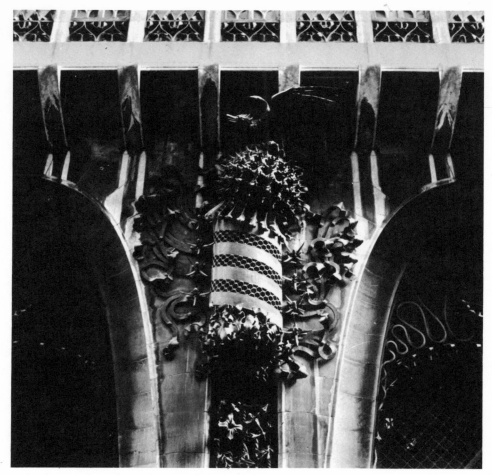

24 Palacio Güell, Barcelona, 1885–9. Escutcheon in high relief between the two gates

25 Palacio Güell, Barcelona Exterior

arched portals. These for the first time are not closed by wooden doors but instead by wrought iron gates which act as a sort of filter, though this innovation, which later became common practice, was at first ill received as if it constituted a sort of civil offence. The relationship with the street was further maintained by the long balcony supported on brackets projecting from the first floor. This again sets as a filter between the interior and the exterior and, by means of the broad windows of the central hall, establishes a direct relationship and a free play of light between the front and rear façades on to the patio, which too takes the form of a veranda and is veiled by translucent ironwork cones.

From one side of the hall one goes down a gentle and beautiful spiral staircase to the stables, where the brick columns which support the building can be seen. From the other one walks up the main stairs to the rooms on the three upper floors, all of which are grouped around the central hall. This was meant for concerts and terminates in a brick paraboloid cupola supported by parabolic arches and surmounted by another, pinnacled cupola which projects through the roof terrace of the palace and is its dominant feature.

It rises at the end of four conical vaults which provide direct illumination to the central hall beyond that provided by the openings in the cupola itself. Around this central protuberance, on the gently sloping roof, a series of conical chimneys create a fairy-tale landscape rich in monochrome and polychrome colorations in enamel, stone, tiles, bricks and many-shaped ceramic tile fragments—all this making up the character of the Palacio Güell, which is not only a rich man's home par excellence but also stands for a new social and cultural attitude. The palace came to represent the characteristic elements of Gaudí's work in Barcelona, leading, like the successive stages in a journey over the city to the final achievement of the Sagrada. Always present as an element in all of Gaudí's other Familia works, it came to represent a symbol of the aspirations of the whole town of Barcelona which found it deeply meaningful.

The parabolic arches of the façade of the Palacio Güell are reiterated in

26 Palacio Güell, Barcelona
Detail of the roof terrace

27 Palacio Güell, Barcelona
Detail of the skylight

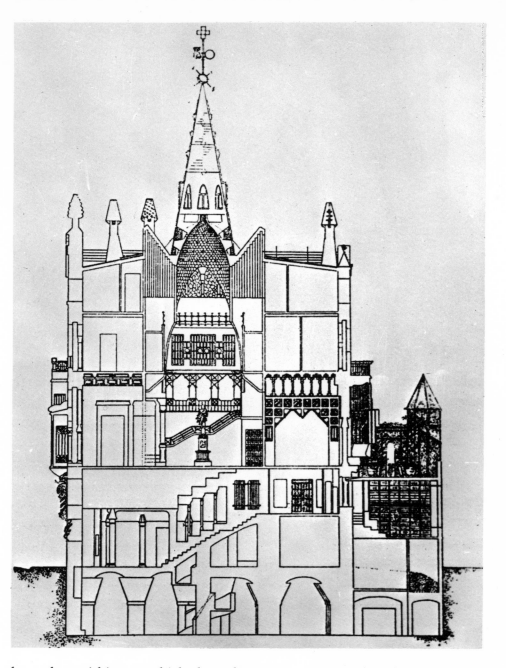

Fig. 25   the arches within, to which the columns are connected with geometrical
motifs based on the hyperbols—already a component of Gaudí's mature
language of expression and one of the first demonstrations of his conception
of architecture as arising from a process of germination and spontaneous
growth, like a natural element.

Gaudí worked on every detail of the palace, from the esutcheon in iron
and in high relief bursting from the wall between the two portals, to the
gratings, ceilings, balustrades, door-knockers and furnishings, trying to
achieve that 'synthesis of the arts' which Morris, Van de Velde and the
Pre-Raphaelites sought to achieve and which can only be found in the work
of extremely gifted artists, at least since the beginning of our technological
civilisation and the onset of specialisation, which has no room for the 'total
artist' in the Classical, Medieval and Renaissance meaning of the term.
This was what the revivalists were after when they wanted to regenerate
certain ideological attitudes, and it is what Ruskin, Morris and the Art
Nouveau movement had sought when trying to set art up as the model for
all technical and industrial activities, believing that art should be a guide to
the taste in man's everyday acts.

In contemporary society cases of artistic synthesis are sometimes found to
be the product of particular artists with more than one facet to their person-
alities (such as Le Corbusier) or are the result of artists collaborating.

Even Gaudí, whose imprint lay so strongly on everything he touched, often requested the collaboration of other artists; for instance that of the painter Clapés, to whom he entrusted some frescoes inside the Palacio Güell and the now faded decoration of an outside wall, as well as the later decoration of Casa Milá; or, later, that of Jujol, who was his refined and sensitive collaborator in the extraordinary and fascinating ceramic mosaics in the Parc Güell and in the ironwork of Casa Milá.

Plates 34, 35

Gaudí had met Clapés in the drawing-room of Eusebio Güell, his extraordinary client, a textile magnate and fervent Catalan nationalist who was broadminded, unprejudiced and had the widest international interests. In his house, artists, musicians, writers and priests rubbed shoulders, and it was probably in his extensive library that Gaudí got to know the works of Ruskin, Morris and the English Pre-Raphaelites; he shared the fervour of the Güell intellectual circle for the music of Wagner.

One might attribute to Gaudí's tireless and disturbed imagination, his fastidiousness, restlessness and compulsion to express himself, the fact that he employed various architectural languages at the same time, sampled the various styles and continuously elaborated on new forms in his desire to find himself and to immerse himself in a broader band of historical time than the age in which he actually lived. Perhaps he was trying to rediscover in the styles of the past some sort of foundation to which he could adhere while discovering new expressive outlets, using the modern techniques available and establishing his own vocabulary. Thus, while he was building the Palacio Güell, he was at the same time planning and carrying out the rebuilding of the Archbishop's Palace at Astorga (1889–93). It had been burned down only a short time previously and the project inspired him to a fantasy world of Gothic; he was drawing up the plans for a pavilion for the Transatlantic Company for the Barcelona Universal Exhibition (1888) in a Moorish style (with what seem like clear references to the Alhambra); he was building the house of Los Botines at León (1891–94) on Gothic lines; he was building the college of the Theresians at Barcelona (1889–94) (where by contrast the architectural formulae are transformed into a 'living language') and above all he was just embarking on the work which, then as now, was to represent the summit of all his ideas and aspirations as builder, artist and believer–the continuation of the expiatory Temple of the Sagrada Familia, whose long drawn out, pondered and polymorphic execution was to coincide with the progressive withdrawal of Gaudí's mind from society and from man. The net of fanatical Catholicism was

Gaudí and Neo-Gothic

29 Project for a hunting lodge for Eusebio Güell at Garraf, Barcelona, 1882

30 Archiepiscopal Palace, Astorga Exterior. 1889–95

31 Design for the façade of the Archiepiscopal Palace at Astorga

drawing itself ever more tightly around him. In this we can see the effects of Counter Reformation introversion, brought about by the temporal powers of the clergy, who held the reins of political power because of the Spaniards' psychological need to spiritualise and exalt certain phenomena to an almost propitiatory end. This remains one of the most strongest reasons for Spain's difficulties in achieving a real democratic liberty. It is also at odds with Spain's intolerance of her own myths, with the national instinct for rebellion and iconoclasm and for the fiesta and the bull-fight, deeply rooted in the Spanish character and racial heritage.

Figs. 30, 31

The rebuilding of the Archbishop's Palace at Astorga was entrusted to Gaudí in 1887 by his countryman Bishop I. B. Grau Vallespinos, while he was still engaged on the Palacio Güell and had already taken over the direction of the continuation of the Sagrada Familia. He tried to reproduce the severe Gothic of northern Europe, but adhered too closely to certain of its stylistic features and evolved an exercise in spatial volumes more complex than the scale of the actual building could permit, thus producing an effect which left little room for the free play of his imagination. This found expression in the great flared hyperbolic arches of the portals, which interact with the perspective-distorting effect of the shadows they cast on themselves, the division of internal spaces, the distortion of planes and the plan for the building's illumination from above. This last project was never realised because, when the Bishop died in 1895, Gaudí was forced to leave Astorga, where he had met with much hostility as a result of his insistence on importing his Catalan workmen, who were already accustomed to his building methods, rather than employing the local artisans.

32 Exterior of Casa de Los Botines, Barcelona, 1892–4

Casa de Los Botines

Fig. 32

The Casa de Los Botines at León, now the home of the local Savings Bank, is built of white granite like the Archbishop's Palace at Astorga and was again based on a neo-Gothic inspiration. However, it evolved as a compact block standing on an irregular rectangular base, a theme which is maintained in the internal layout.

The characteristic of the precise demarcation of space is strong in Gaudí's version of Neo-Gothic and sets him apart from practically all his Revivalist contemporaries. One of the characteristics of the revival is that buildings are treated as if they have only one dimension, in the sense that they consist only of elevations. These often bear little relation to each other, as if each one were drawn from a nineteenth-century print or oleograph. However, in Gaudí's work, space always intervenes: whatever the façade, it has its outer layer and its inner layer joined by solid matter in between.

In the Casa de Los Botines the openings for the windows are progressively wider towards the base of the building. On the first floor they take the form of closely spaced triforium openings (recalling, perhaps, albeit indirectly, a characteristic of Venetian architecture). Another notable feature is the use of iron in the railings of the portal and in the railing which encircles the buildings and filters the light which enters the windows of the semi-basement.

College of the Theresians

But Gaudí's most interesting work of this period is undoubtedly the college of the Theresians in Barcelona, in which the limitations of the means at his disposal left no room for his usual elaborate decoration and instead fostered the evolution of a clear and precise plan in which the use of Gothic features, such as the white cloistered corridors with their parabolic arches endowed with all the purity of certain Gothic interiors, gave rise to an intense expressiveness full of peace and tranquillity seldom found elsewhere in Gaudí's work, which is usually taut and never replete, as if he had a sort of 'horror vacui'.

Plates 14, 15

Plate 13

The austere exterior displays a rhythmic use of its two facing materials, brick and raw stone, exemplifying the particular feeling Gaudí brought to all his facing of walls. The rhythm is maintained by the central projection which rises above the beautiful iron gate of the doorway, by the battlements

surrounding the roof and by the lively angular features. The interior is perfectly coherent with the rest of the building; the layout is simple and it corresponds exactly with the exterior. This work is impressive for its reserved and severe intimacy as well as for its proud and concentrated expressive force, which is further emphasised by its unusual complete lack of ornamentation.

A project

A commission to build a home for the Franciscan Mission in Tangiers (1892–93) provided the impetus for Gaudí, who had always obstinately refused to move from Barcelona (it will be recalled that he had not even gone to Comillas to supervise the building of El Capricho) to visit Andalusia and North Africa, in the company of the Marquis of Comillas (Eusebio Güell's brother-in-law), who had given him the commission. Even though this project never materialised, it remains a fact that the African experience was a landmark in Gaudí's development in that the local architecture he saw sparked off an idea for the spires of his Sagrada Familia. Originally these had been designed as conical, but they were eventually to be hyperboloid.

Casa Calvet

With the Casa Calvet, built between 1898 and 1904 in Calle de Caspe, Barcelona, Gaudí's intentions altered inasmuch as he wanted to combine Baroque with modernist features. The Baroque element is supplied by the upper double-curved projections to the façade which rise above the roof

34 Tower of Bellesguard,
Barcelona, 1900–2
Detail of the *desván* (attic)

terrace and are pierced by two small open balconies and by the rich ironwork
decoration of the curving balconies and the veranda above the central portal.
Plate 19   The 'modernist' element is supplied by the spatial layout of the interior, certain of the facing materials employed, and by some of the furnishings. The
lift cage, interpreted as an element of dynamic plasticity, shows a wealth
of invention and an incredible abundance of forged and traceried ironwork.
One should note also the details of the elaborate outside door-knocker and
Plate 22   its spy-hole, as well as the details of the knocker on the inner entrance door
and the 'rocaille' tubs on the inner terrace. But perhaps the most notable
Fig. 33   'moderna' feature is the 'functionalist' design of the rear façade, with continuous glazed bands, regularly spaced and integrated by balconies which
in turn provide some ornamental relief.

Bellesguard
Fig. 10
Plates 23, 25

While the fantasy of a minareted city was the dominant feature of the design
for the home of the Franciscan Mission at Tangiers, it was a kind of fairy-tale
Gothic that moulded the tower of Bellesguard, which Gaudí built between
1900 and 1902 at No. 46 Calle de Bellesguard, Barcelona, near the river
Vilana. The tower was erected in memory of King Martin I of Aragon who
had had a residence on the same spot. Thus, with the aim of setting up the
ruins of the old royal residence on the land adjacent to the tower and so
including the ruins in the garden, Gaudí had a street diverted to the banks of
the Vilana. This gave him the opportunity to construct his first vaulting with
inclined columns instead of leaning walls, to hold back the embankment.

28

35 Finca Miralles, Las Corts
de Sarria, Barcelona, 1901
Part of the boundary wall

36 Gateway of the Finca Miralles,
Las Corts de Sarria, Barcelona

A striking later example of this vaulting was its successful application in the Parc Güell.

The edifice is topped by a tall angular spire crowned with a four-branched cross (a feature which might be regarded as a Gaudian signature), and is completely covered outside by fragments of stone in a most delicate chromatic relationship with each other. Windows of various shapes pierce the walls at irregular intervals corresponding to the layout of the rooms, which is among Gaudí's most interesting designs. The interior is entirely of brick, covered with stucco, with rounded corners in the stairs and rooms and a rhythmic play in the arrangement of columns, pilasters and bracketed arches in an imaginative play of rational but very bold structural forms. This is illustrated in the *desván* (attic), where slender pilasters, two bricks thick, open out as they rise to meet a platform constructed of two layers of brick, twenty-two bricks wide and two bricks deep. This platform supports the lobed vaulting which in turn supports the roof. Other characteristic features include an external drainpipe covered with stone chips, the intricate ironwork of the gate with its *coup de fouet* pediment consistent with the best traditions of Art Nouveau, and the stained glass relief star, a radiant kaleidoscopic image, placed above the stair-well window.

Fig. 34

Plate 24

Meanwhile (1901), he was busy with the construction of the wall and entrance gate of the Finca Miralles at Las Corts de Sarvia, near the Finca Güell. The architect Sugranes was also working on this, under Gaudí's guidance. The wall itself is made of stone, curving both horizontally and vertically, and is crowned by an iron railing which repeats this motion in a sort of counterpoint. In the gate, whose roof is the work of Sugranes, one should note the serpentine plasticity of the arches and the lateral railing, in which Gaudí evolved the motif of the linear superimposition of two opposed series of curved lines moving in parallel directions.

Finca Miralles
Fig. 35

Fig. 36

We come now to one of the most brilliant, unrestrained and yet most controlled and rational works of art of our century—the Parc Güell. It was built between 1900 and 1914 as a sort of setting for a garden city. Once again it was Eusebio Güell who, following the setting up of a Garden City association in London in 1899, gave Gaudí the commission.

The park occupies the district of the Muntayana Pelada near the slopes of Tibidabo and looks directly across Barcelona to the sea. It had been envisaged as a site for sixty dwellings, each surrounded by a garden, but this scheme fell through and the park was given to the city and became open to the public.

The Parc Güell
Plates 26–35
Figs. 37–39

37 Tree-columns in
the Parc Güell, Barcelona, 1900–14

38 Tree-columns in
the Parc Güell, Barcelona, 1900–14

While Gaudí's feelings for nature and his desire to reproduce its creative processes are evident in every detail of this work, it should not be thought that it was an instinct to imitate nature which drove Gaudí towards this fanciful creation, nor that any part of this enormous work with its infinite variations and creations was left to chance or to an uncontrolled and unbridled imagination. Every apparent liberty in this vast panorama, in which stone is used in trees, branches and spongey bushes to become a natural organic element, is in reality the result of precise calculation, governed by strict rules of balancing and counterbalancing forces and loads and impulses.

There is no architectural creation, however full of fantasy (and the park is in every detail the result of a continuous process of imaginative creation), that is not based on sound principles of construction. It would seem that here Gaudí's characteristic boundless invention directed itself towards technological rationality to the extent that it almost became an end in itself. A sort of rational mania and desire to exploit daring technological solutions at all costs almost to the point of extravagance might perhaps be explained by the suggestion that he might have been afraid of not being in touch with the latest technological discoveries. Dutert's famous Machinery Hall with its triple-articulated arch, 115 metres wide, at the Paris Exhibition had been built in 1889, and Gaudí's efforts look primitive and archaic by comparison. In fact, this apparent insecurity about technical advancement was in a way irrelevant, as Gaudí's real aim was achieved exclusively through expression.

A study of the constants in Gaudí's creative work, and in particular his tendency towards entwined, radiating, parabolic and 'agglutinate' forms would probably confirm his tireless cerebral activity. I use the word 'agglutinate' advisedly as a term from the realm of psychiatry, appropriately from the study in pathology of some graphic representations. I do not wish to introduce the question of Gaudí as a case of psychoanalysis, although these researches might prove quite illuminating. But such researches would be useful in that they would help us to avoid the errors and misapprehensions, which have often arisen about works of art in which the psychological elements are most evident, as in an artist like Van Gogh.

To affirm in this way, in the interests of a critical assessment, that certain researches might lead one astray, makes it all the more important to study them as closely as all the other documents and sources of information. This

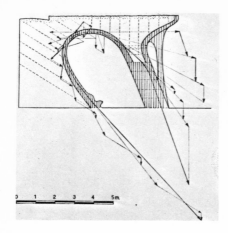

39 Sectional drawing of a curved walk on a viaduct in the Parc Güell, with indications of loads and impulses

one can do only by taking the aspects of his work individually.

The Parc Güell covers thirty-eight acres and comprises streets, viaducts and paths of various gradients, taking full advantage of the natural terrain and characteristics of the mountainside. This continuous respect for nature and the reconstruction of nature's creations gives weight to the argument that the Parc Güell should be interpreted as the most fully-developed expression of sixteenth- and seventeenth-century landscape architecture and, particularly, the tradition of the English garden. There are certainly various references in it, but I would concur with Ragghianti[23] in seeing it primarily as an extension of Italian and French fifteenth-century architecture—perhaps even by way of Palissy—although I think Buontalenti is more important than Ammanati, the source which Ragghianti suggested. Roberto Pane[24] points out a more patent reference to 'ancient and complex structures which make use of the conformations of rock on site to make walls and arches which are primitive and ingenuous but at the same time ingenious' in Catalonia itself and in the Balearics, from Tarragona to the *barracas* of Majorca and Minorca.

However, Gaudí's rapport with nature is too direct and too profoundly felt for any attempt to be made to justify any indirect cultural reference. Indeed, if there is one phase in Gaudí's career when any suggestion of a cultural cross-reference can be entirely forgotten, it is the Parc Güell, provided one overlooks the naïve and perhaps ironic presence of the squat Doric columns supporting the big end terrace. These columns are unique in Gaudí's work, even though he was later to call the Nativity door of the Sagrada Familia '*grieco*' (Greek).

One enters the Parc Güell by the two resplendent fairy-tale pavilions, which dazzle the eye with the colours reflecting from their ceramic surfaces and changing as the sun moves round the sky, and culminate in highly ornate blue and white spires. Then one finds oneself in a sort of enchanted garden, welcomed by the enormous lizard-dragon, covered with majolica, which lies along the balustrade of the double staircase. At the top of these steps stand a great flared entrance arch, a fountain and, in the background, the great Doric colonnade which accentuates the sense of disquiet provoked by its irrational presence and by the leaning of its columns. This could be taken as an anticipation of Pop, but it is really on the level of Kitsch or Disneyland. In fact, there can be no question of a direct influence; these are only analogies which may assist in the understanding of a cultural moment.

But perhaps Gaudí is playing games with us in this landscape architecture. For example the accentuation of the pointed verticality of the stones in the leaning columns and in the arches of the viaducts and the sense of vertigo deliberately provoked in the curving paths, shown in the section-drawing with its diagram of loads and thrusts. The path runs on, propped up on sharply leaning tree-like columns, and twists back violently towards the terrace, where the wall emphasises the curve of the opposed columns. Here again we might find a reference to the jokes of eighteenth-century gardens such as labyrinths, *trompe-l'œil* and hidden fountains, but Gaudí's is a game that is, so to speak, entirely in the mind.

The question of games in Gaudí's architecture comes up again in the marvellous mosaic decoration on the serpentine parapet of the children's game terrace, in which Gaudí had the sensitive and genial collaboration of Jujol (the creator of, among other things, the beautiful ceramic decorations of the ceiling of the Doric hall). Here we have one of Gaudí's most free and happy creations, which does not appear to have any cultural pre-occupations. He seems, moreover, to have achieved a perfect balance between invention and reason as well as the relaxation and self-realisation which were his intangible dream. This particular work has a joyousness and spontaneity which many other of his colourful fairyland creations have, but which

Fig. 39

Plates 34, 35

23 C. L. Ragghianti, *A.G.*, in 'Sele Arte' no. 35, 1958.
24 R. Pane, *Op. Cit.*

40 Drawing for the iron canopy
for the interior of
the Cathedral of Majorca, 1904–14

they seem to want to impose on us forcibly, provoking a sensation of estrangement and alienation which often leaves us perplexed.

Gaudí worked on the restoration of the Cathedral of Majorca between 1904 and 1914. His work there was called a *reforma* ('reformation') in Spanish texts, a 'liturgical architectural restoration' by Rafols[25] and a problem was posed as to the legitimacy of direct alteration, rather than mere consolidation and conservation, in the repairing of ancient monuments. This is a complex problem and one to which no general rule can be applied. Brandi states that alteration of ancient works of art is no longer probable in the modern age (that is, the past 150 years) because it is today that the 'historical consciousness of the monument' and hence the 'necessary recognition of the irreversible status of the present historical consciousness' is re-emerging, which 'hinders us from interfering with monuments from the past'.[26] If this is so, then it is also true that there are no breaks in history, that its course is irreversible and that our artistic heritage must therefore not be mummified. Churches and monuments have a continuing history – they are not museums. (There would also, and to a greater extent, be the problem of the cocooning and crystallisation of all ancient cities, which would be more or less equivalent to burying them.) No one situation, however, is quite like another and every individual case must be judged not according to an established principle, but scientifically and by means of critical analysis.

In the case of this liturgical architectural restoration by Gaudí, which has aroused so much fuss and disagreement, we are confronted with a work which bears a definite personal stamp but is neither disrespectful nor at variance with its surroundings. It is limited to the insertion of ironwork diaphragms and glass for the apse windows (in which he used three super-

Architectural restoration

Fig. 40

25 J. F. Rafóls, *A.G.*, Barcelona, 1960.
26 C. Brandi, *L'inserzione del nuovo nel vecchio*, in *Op. Cit.*

imposed sheets of coloured glass to obtain the various shades, as in three-colour printing), the creation of the beautiful hanging canopy and the lighting of the basilica. It might be added that this was not a job that could be casually entrusted to just anybody, as is demonstrated by the absolutely intolerable glass later put in by an anonymous person.

According to Bergós,[27] Gaudí said of his work on the Cathedral of Majorca: 'Let us have architecture without archaeology; our primary consideration is the relationship between the parts as they stand; therefore we do not copy their shapes but produce forms of a predetermined character possessing the spirit of the original.' This seems to be a direct criticism of the whole spectrum of nineteenth-century restoration based on arbitrary archaeological refurbishing in the manner of Viollet-le-Duc.

The crypt of Santa Coloma   Gaudí's mastery of structural laws and static equilibrium led him to a freer

27 Bergós, *Op. Cit.*

expression of fantasy to the extent that every problem seems to have been deliberately provoked, purely for the joy of solving it. One may take this as another application of the 'games' concept in Gaudí's work, and may find evidence of it in the crypt of the chapel of the Colonia Güell. The Colonia was a housing estate for workers at Cervelló near Barcelona, built between 1898 and 1915. Güell, the great industrialist and patron, commissioned Gaudí to design a number of buildings to provide social services for the workers, among which was the chapel. The crypt, although incomplete, represents one of Gaudí's greatest achievements. It was in this work that Gaudí, with a new freedom, first applied the new structural theories by means of which he sought to avoid the Gothic tripartite structure. By adhering once again to the laws of natural growth, he achieved archaic and barbaric shapes of an intense and dramatic expressiveness by a natural rather than a cultural process. The chromatic relationships based on the mingling of various materials such as coloured stones, brick, basalt, cement, iron, enamel and stained glass produced a concentration of fantasy which the right light-

Figs. 41–46

41–46 Crypt of the chapel of Sta Coloma, Cervelló, Barcelona, 1898–1915. 41 detail of the exterior; 42, 43 details of the interior of the crypt;

ing, which Gaudí certainly planned, would have heightened and intensified. Its absolute independence from Revivalism and of any formal preconceptions, inasmuch as the work is born of the total of Gaudí's experience, not a lot of individual sources, above all, the freedom of every decorative feature make this crypt an incomparable vehicle of emotional expression. It is to this most pure example of faith in the potential of man's creative fantasy that many have turned in a desire to re-create the same mystico-religious symbolism, in doing which Gaudí succeeded in reviving the most authentic Gothic spiritual condition. (The example comes to mind of the Expressiveness of Michelucci's Chiesa dell'Autastrada.) If one looks at the highly elaborate preparatory studies and the splendid funicular models which Gaudí used to experiment with loads and thrusts and to determine the angle of the columns and pilasters, one gets some idea of the great clarity of his vision and of the transformation that the technical aspects underwent in the course of his planning, eventually becoming one with the fantasy. Gaudí's models rather resembled mobiles before their time: to the ceiling of his studio he attached a series of wires along the length of which he hung small weights proportional to the calculated loads of the vaulting. Then he photographed the model and elaborated the design on the photograph. A study of Gaudí's plans

44 (page 36) funicular model (upside-down) of the arches;
45 sketch of the chapel;
46 view from outside

47 Casa Battló, Barcelona, 1905–7. Details of the exterior

48 Casa Battló, Barcelona
Detail of the crest of the roof

49 Casa Battló, Barcelona. A room

50 Casa Battló, Barcelona
Exterior

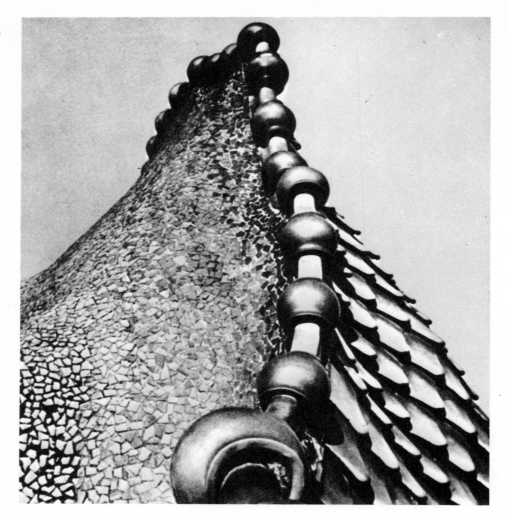

for vaulting in such photographs might enable one to identify some of the characteristics of Guarini's architecture in Gaudí's projective geometry.

That it should not have been Gaudí himself who invented the use of the catenary curve in checking the static curve of an arch (one should perhaps bear in mind that Ammanati's Ponte Santa Trinita in Florence is also based on the catenary curve) does not seem to me to detract from the originality and validity of Gaudí's working method.

Casa Battló

Figs. 47, 50

Fig. 48
Fig. 47

In this all too brief analysis of Gaudí's work, it is scarcely possible to make a close study of Casa Battló in Calle de Aragona, Barcelona, on which Gaudí worked between 1905 and 1907. This is because of the complexity of the themes presented and the closely linked relationship between the exterior and the interior, which together form one of the most perfect examples of a sculptural 'organism'. One need only look at the refined shaping of the façade, where a delicate chromatic effort and skilful chiaroscuro are very much in evidence towards the base of the building. The façade rises towards the green, dominating and shining scaled crest of the sloping roof, the first-floor terrace projecting with its moulded apertures and central bone-like columns. '*Casa de los huesos*' (house of bones) is one of the popular names for Casa Battló. But every organic reference is in fact overshadowed by the playful, almost eighteenth-century masks of the balconies above. Another popular name for the Casa Battló is 'house of masks'. The scattered polychrome of the exterior, strewn with blobs and drops as if handfuls of coloured confetti have been thrown at it, evokes the atmosphere of a Venetian carnival with gondolas and crinolines. One should note also the water motif of the reflective surface and of the noble crest, resembling the beak of a Venetian state barge.

Thus a lightness of touch and a gay nonchalance are apparent, while the

METRO

CORRESP NCIA RENFE

rational element is still there. The structure has the function whereby in its complex arrangements, every external element is inextricably bound up in the slow, flexible and uninterrupted development of the whole organism. From the main staircase, entirely shaped by hand, where it is possible for the first time to find precise formal analogies with the linguistic modes of a certain Surrealist magic, such as was evoked by Miró and Arp, to the splendid luminescent rooms, one feels the presence of a single and continuous moulding force which never gets out of control. It is present in the gentle movement of the walls embellished with chiaroscuro, as it is in the ample and subtle spirals of the ceilings, the rounded corners and the surfaces on which the light plays.

Fig. 49

Roberto Pane quotes a phrase, attributed to Gaudí, which seems to stand out here as the symbol of a happy and established equilibrium: 'The corners and angles will disappear and the matter will show itself abundant in astral roundness; the sun will penetrate on all four sides and it will be the image of paradise. The contrasts will make my palace more luminous than light.'[28]

One should note how this beautiful façade adapts itself to that of the fine house adjacent to it, the Casa Amattler, designed by Puig i Cadafach. (On the other hand, the building on the other side has been made two storeys higher, without consideration for Casa Battló, to very bad effect.) Look too at the majolica-encrusted spire bearing the usual four-branched cross, the dazzling crest of the roof which symbolises a mountain peak in Montserrat and is edged with a series of enlarged green ceramic 'pearls'. Inside there are two skylights lined with tiles which bring light towards the centre of the house and are separated from the sky by windows supported on parabolic beams. The rear façade has vertical glazed bands recalling the rear façade of Casa Calvet. And the roof carries a compact group of majolica-studded chimneys which are not visible from the front of the house but which anticipate the fantastic, vigilant and disturbing presences on the roof-terrace of 'La Pedrera'—the Casa Milá.

La Pedrera

Plate 36
Figs. 51–53

In the Casa Milá, known as 'La Pedrera' (stone quarry), which he built between 1905 and 1910, Gaudí brought to its peak his conception of the work of architecture as a sculptural organism, compact and uninterrupted. In the Palacio Güell, he had already ceased to make a positive distinction between the various elements of the columns and arches, making the capital and arch grow directly out of the column. In the Parc Güell also one can see this idea at work in the spiralling columns which, growing broader with each successive wave, fill and create the vault. Casa Milá is like an enormous lump of fused stone, retaining all the impurities, bubbles and lumps of the stone. It is this oneness moulded as if by hand in clay and then solidified in lava, which makes this work resemble the form of so much modern European sculpture (like for instance an enormous and immobile reclining figure by Henry Moore). It also showed Gaudí as an Expressionist ten or fifteen years before the impact of Expressionism was felt. The Einstein tower at Potsdam by Mendelsohn dates from 1920; Finsterlin's, Poelzig's and Bruno Taut's projects date from 1919–20. It is important to recognise how advanced Gaudí was.

Gaudí conceived La Pedrera as a public monument to the Virgin of the Rosary, whose statue was to have stood at the top, transforming the building into a great compact mountain of rock above which the image was to rise towards the sky. For this reason he never considered this building complete. He left its completion in the hands of Jujol and Clapés and abandoned it when his client, preoccupied by the disorders in Barcelona in the famous 'tragic week' of 1909, asked him to give up the idea of putting the enormous statue on the roof, suggesting that the building would easily get mistaken for a convent, thus arousing the wrath of the iconoclastic revolutionaries.

Be that as it may, this immense organism with its undulating forms remains a unique and marvellous example of the expressive strength of

28 R. Pane, *Op. Cit.*

40

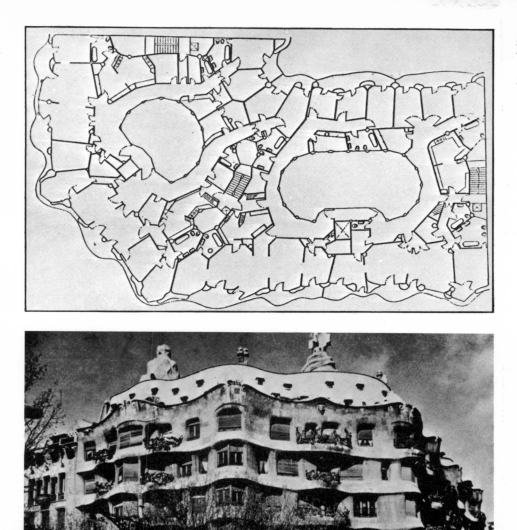

51 Plan of the Casa Milá,
Barcelona

52 Casa Milá, Barcelona. Exterior

Gaudí's vision and of his ability to anticipate stylistic forms which more recent technical progresses ultimately rendered feasible.

As always, Gaudí evolved such advanced forms using traditional methods, in his customary desire to demonstrate the possibility of applying new methods to old instruments. Naturally this process involved the need to conquer the material's resistance to new applications and the difficulty of inventing ever more expressive uses for the materials. One need only stop to think of the devices which he had to employ in order to express his ideas in this new building, using huge blocks of stone rather than concrete. He had also to make use of a sort of reinforced brick, which he also used in the Parc Güell, to make this dynamic structure firm, for it was based entirely around the movement of the parabolic and hyperbolic arch, which he employs in an entirely new and free fashion. Indeed, by using parabolic and hyperbolic arches, he achieved an extraordinary effect in the horizontal lines in relief which encircle the building and cause the totality of the planes to refract itself analytically, thus provoking the almost physical diffraction of the undulating horizontal line. It looks as if he had produced the plan in elevation and had synthesised it at the meeting of the planes. This was almost the reverse of Borromini's experiment in the façade of San Carlino. Borromini had revealed the continuous line as the ultimate limit of Baroque;

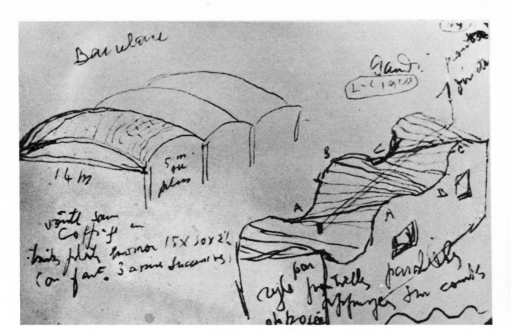

53 Casa Milá, Barcelona
Detail of the chimneys
on the roof terrace

54 Drawing made by Le Corbusier
in 1928 of the roof of the school
of the Sagrada Familia,
Barcelona, 1909

55 School of the Sagrada Familia,
Barcelona, 1909

Gaudí rediscovered it in order to use it to give the architectural mass a readable coherent formal component (as he had with the tight, created curve of the balcony in the Parc Güell).

Standing on massive columns (there is a garage underneath) which let light through right to the ground, Casa Milá's finest feature is its great continuous projecting bands interspersed with plant-like entwined ironwork railings which filter the light falling on the surfaces of the building. These sometimes extend the balconies on to the flat surfaces of the horizontal bands, which advance and recede and permit the light to filter through to the floors below.

Elsewhere the projecting band is lower than the level of the rooms in order to make a clear view of the street possible. This is an interesting instance of Gaudí's intuitive understanding of the communicative and extrovert character of town life. It is also one which may even seem strange in an artist such as Gaudí, who was closed and introverted in character.

While the Casa Milá is also interesting for the free development of its internal layout, its outstanding feature lies in the rich, unsuspected and fabulous complexity of its roof-terrace, peopled with the creations of Gaudí's fantasy—chimneys bursting with colour, skylights, and the roofs covering the stairs leading out to the terrace—all these creating a disturbing and dramatic landscape. Here Gaudí has conjured up monsters, and one cannot fail to notice Gaudí's vision of the things which were to explode on to the art scene a few years later; the anguish of German Expressionism is embodied in the presentiment of terrible wars represented by the warrior monsters in the form of Saracens, Teutonic knights, warriors from outer space, robots in pursuit like horrible death-machines and the tragic Munch-like mask of a human scream.

With its network of iron railings and barriers this is a nightmare landscape, a sort of Auschwitz, and what is staggering is that Gaudí achieved it all without once resorting to anthropomorphic or naturalistic means of representation. These immense totems are based entirely on the conjunction of geometric forms and on continual variations on the paraboloid, the helicoid and the hyperboloid, which are the fundamental structural nuclei of these forms that seem to take on a lifelike quality.

The Sagrada Familia is the colossal work in which Gaudí saw the fulfilment of his mission as architect, builder, believer and creator. Like Dante he imagined that his mission was to emulate God by creating a microcosm using the images of the macrocosm. But before we turn to this gigantic phenomenon, a word must be said about one of Gaudí's last and most perfect works—

Fig. 51
Fig. 53

The School of the Sagrada Familia

56 Drawings by Bergós of
the third and fourth phases in
the design of the Sagrada Familia
in Barcelona, 1891–1926

57 Interior of the apse of
the Expiatory Temple of
the Sagrada Familia, Barcelona

the little School of the Sagrada Familia. This was built in 1909 and there is now some talk of demolishing it for reasons of town-planning, which is only yet another scandal in our society which has protested loudly about the destruction of historic monuments in the past and does little or nothing to stop it now. Its fate will probably be the same as that of Horta's Maison du Peuple in Brussels, which was demolished with the promise that it would be erected elsewhere; and that of the Scottish medieval castles, dismantled piece by piece, packaged, and shipped off to America by so many rich industrialists—complete with their ghosts.

Fig. 55

However, suffice it to say that the little School of the Sagrada Familia is one of Gaudí's most perfectly balanced works and that it would be impossible to set it up anywhere else. It is based on the application of the hyperbolic arch and vault, and this feature is carried right through from the undulating walls with their small windows to the alternating slopes of the subtly vaulted roof. The latter effect is obtained through the dynamic evolution of the hyperbole; there are several rectangular sections, each pivoting on the same central axis, with the result that when one end of a section is raised, the other is lowered, producing a convex shape at one end and a concave shape at the other. (One is reminded of the exercises which Gabo, Pevsner, Moholy-Nagy and others made in the study of the dynamics of linear elements.) The result is a small but complex and self-sufficient organism, compact and at the same time lively and pleasing—probably because Gaudí conceived of its geometry not as an abstract exercise, but as an effort to adhere to the laws of natural and organic structures.

The roof of the school, which is covered with thin tiles laid in overlapping foliate patterns, looks like the work of a hand guided inexorably by natural forces, and one can see why Le Corbusier was so interested in it. He in fact

Fig. 54

made a sketch of the school illustrating this principle.

The Expiatory Temple of the Sagrada Familia

The Sagrada Familia poses a great many apparently insoluble problems. Firstly and above all there is the question of its completion, for Gaudí's imprint on it goes so deep that intervention by another hand would be impossible. Beyond this it would be difficult to carry out Gaudí's plans and ideas exactly as he would have wanted them because he was constantly altering features and inserting new ones while actually on site at the time they were being built. The completion of the building would only result in the mummification of original idea born live in Gaudí's imagination but, without his life force, still-born in reality. There is also the question of the legitimacy of such an operation, in aesthetic and critical terms, and even, now and then, in terms of religion. Although the Gothic spirit sprang from a community feeling, and Gaudí achieved an understanding of it on a personal level, and it is touching that the people of a city should insist, in a spirit of collective dedication, on furthering this project, it can no longer be assumed that, in our times, a community spirit will necessarily be authentic or lasting after its initial impetus. Nevertheless, apart from the parts of this inspiring building actually directed by Gaudí, we still have a great quantity of his preparatory drawings and models (many of these were destroyed during the Civil War in 1936 but have since been rebuilt). They give us proof of Gaudí's perpetual inventive activity and his incessant struggle to give ever freer expression to his interpretation of the Gothic spirit; 'for this reason we do not copy the forms, but we are able to endow them with a precise character which retains their spirit'.

He spent many years working on the Sagrada Familia. It might even be said that from a certain moment, from about 1914 onwards, right to the end of his life, he no longer concerned himself with anything else, although even in this one can see a certain amount of will to react against events in Europe and the world, albeit in an introverted and fanatical way. He shut himself up in a small room on the site offices of the building and lived only for his 'object', determined never, even in physical terms, to be separated from it, for it had become his dominant preoccupation, appearing now perhaps as

58 View of the interior
of the reconstructed model
of the Sagrada Familia, Barcelona

his sole salvation. This attitude is reflected in the complex religious symbolism to which every minute detail of the building is subordinated. It is reflected too, in the wish implicit in the actual name of the temple, now an expiratory legacy for Gaudí's posterity.

He himself had inherited it. It had been begun in 1882 by Francisco de Paula del Villar, who had been given the commission by José Matia Bocabella, a well-known Barcelona bookseller who had bought the land and championed the cause for the construction of a church dedicated to St Joseph (his own name) and to the Holy Family, which was to be the emblem of the rebirth of the city.

The building Paula del Villar was started as a Neo-Gothic one, and he set to work on the crypt, but after a few months he had disagreements with Martorell, Bocabella's architect and adviser, and abandoned the project. Thus it was that Martorell, who did not wish to take over the entire operation himself, suggested the name of Gaudí, then thirty, who took over the continuation of the church on November 3rd, 1883. He incorporated into the Sagrada Familia all the structural innovations he had developed through this desire to 'correct' the 'errors' of Gothic, ridding it of those flying buttresses – 'crutches' (*les muletas*) as he called them – by transferring the loads formerly carried by these buttresses to columns within the building, angled so as to take the necessary stresses, and looking like trees, with branches and shoots – explosions of decorative structure which once again seem to achieve a Pop enlargement of nature.

Figs. 56, 58

The Sagrada Familia was conceived as a great mystical poem, full of allusions, and a detailed and coherent symbolism which is closely bound up with the rules of the liturgy. By the end of his life, Gaudí had built, apart from the crypt, the portal of the Nativity and the four soaring bell-towers of the façade, which rise from the middle of Barcelona like enigmatic symbols, 'multi-coloured and brilliant in the sun. Their fantasy and distance from reality are in direct contrast to the tangle of natural forms which move and swarm in the unexpected enchanted forest of the decoration of the portal. This contrast is particularly appreciated by lovers of the bizarre; they reel in ecstasy before this strange Baroque blossoming, from which rise large figures whose disconcerting naturalism is a little macabre and always cold and lifeless. We know that Gaudí drew these likenesses from immediate reality in so far as he paid for moulds to be taken from living figures, thus heightening the disturbing contrast between dream and reality, between the definitely dead and the live. It is a feature which is founded on an ambiguity because, in fact, it is in the reality that he imagined that we find life, and those parts which are faithful copies of living beings, still palpitating in their moulds, are absolutely dead.'[29]

Plates 37–40

These words of Perucho's are, in the final analysis, equally applicable to the continuation, by means of 'moulds', of a work which, precisely because it evolved along the lines it did, can never really have any further vital extension. This is already implicit in the hallucinated world of Gaudí's introversion, that 'cerebral productivity', which as has been seen, impelled Gaudí on to ever more spectacular and daring feats of structural virtuosity.

In his latest volume[30] Bohigas speaks of the 'obsessive vocabulary which often became absurdly confining'. 'It is then', he adds, 'that he moves away from the European avant-garde cultural line. Fascinated with speculation about form, he forgets fundamental architectural problems. Around 1920 the most appropriate thing for him to do was to correct the naive and archaic symbolism of the temple and to realise the patent absurdity of continuing the construction of a church with five naves and an impenetrable forest of columns, and to arrive at a more sensible division of the space. He might have done all these things had he been at the creative peak which produced La Pedrera and the Colonia Güell.' This is an observation with which I do

---

29 J. Perucho-L. Pomés, *Op. Cit.*
30 O. Bohigas, *Op. Cit.*

not feel I agree, for it should not be forgotten that the Sagrada Familia represented to Gaudí a sort of total synthesis of all his work and that he wanted to achieve in it the sum of his architecture so far as its powers of expression were concerned. Bohigas says that 'in those years Gropius and Meyer had already built the Fagus Factory (1911); J. J. P. Oud, the first workers' houses in Rotterdam (1920); Le Corbusier, the pavilion of the Esprit Nouveau (1925); Breuer had made the first steel tube-framed chair (1925), and Gropius had opened the Bauhaus at Dessau (1926)'. These facts are true enough, but they can lead to a misunderstanding of Gaudí's entire work, for architecture had always been for him above all else a means for the expression of fantasy and emotion, in spite of (or even by means of) the structural virtuosity of his work.

The main and vital features of Gaudí's work were his inexhaustible and obsessive search for expression, his desire to resolve the representative function of architecture in its day-to-day applications, and his success in regaining for man the meaning of an artistic field which gives man an opportunity to exalt himself beyond the level of his ordinary existence.

Colour plates

4

7

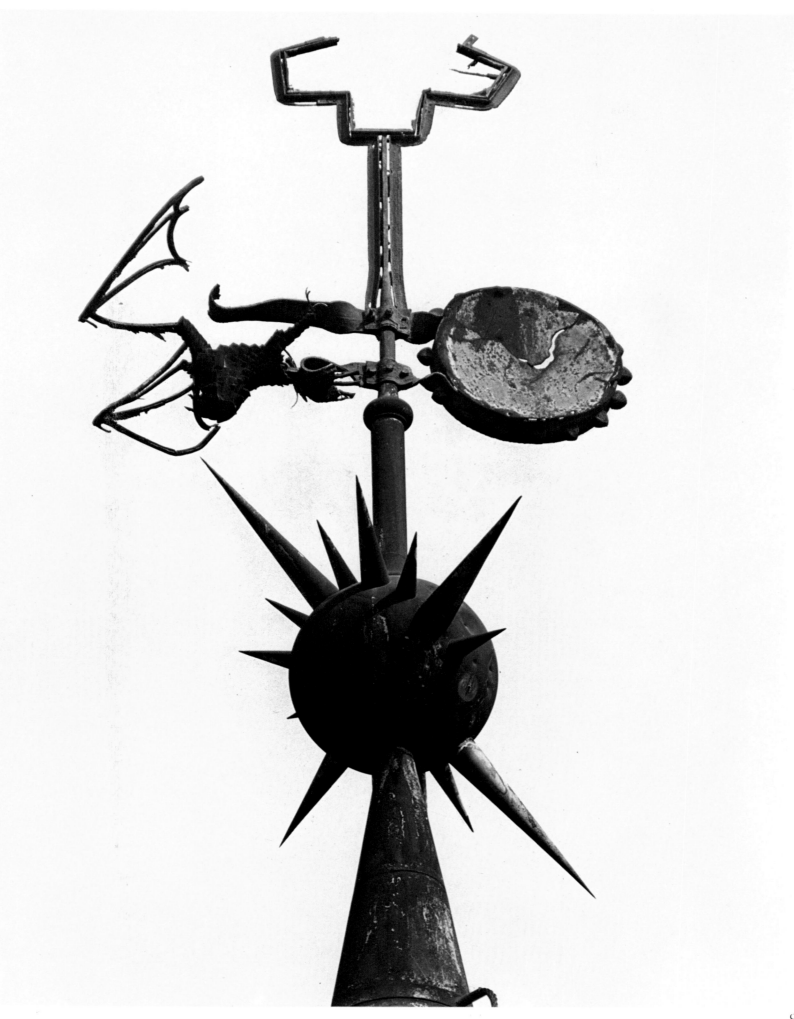

12

13

14

18

20

26

28

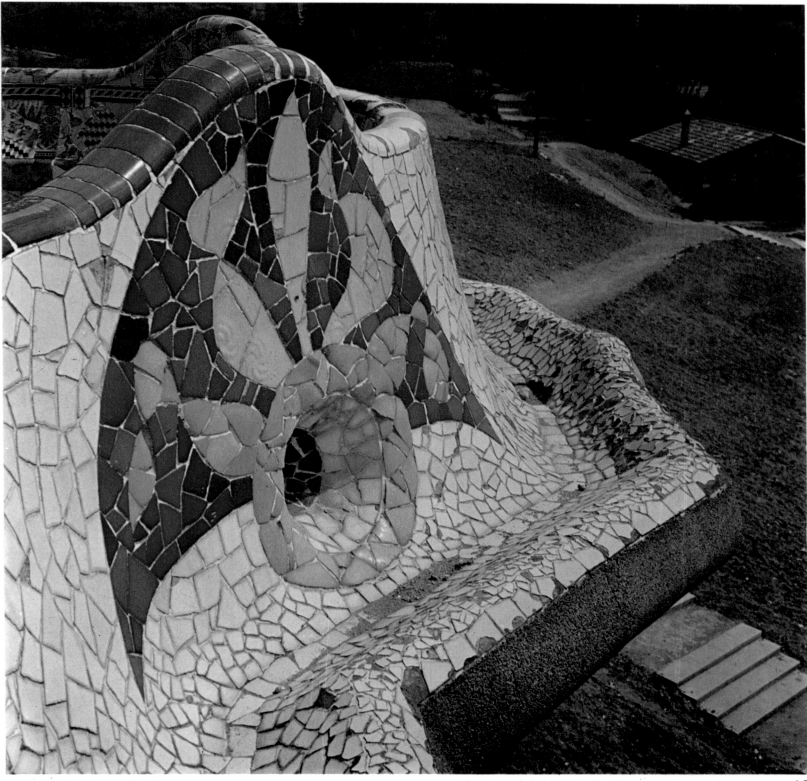

40

Description of colour plates

Biographical notes

A number of documents unearthed by Guix Sugrañes of Reus seem to favour Reus, a town in the Campo de Tarragona, as the place where Antoni Gaudí y Cornet was born on 25th June, 1852–a privilege claimed also by the neighbouring town of Riudoms. In fact it appears that before 1870 there was no record of births in the district. However, Gaudí's baptism was registered at Reus on 26th June in the same year.

His father and forefathers were coppersmiths, and he always laid great stress on the importance of his artisan origins, as if they were a principal reason for his tendency to think in terms of space. He lost his mother when still a child; she gave him his second name–Cornet. While still very young, he also lost his brother and sister, and took charge of his sister's orphaned daughter, Rosa Igea, who stayed with him until his death. He first went to school at Reus and in 1869 went to Barcelona, where he passed the entrance examinations into the new School of Architecture at the University. He took his diploma in 1878.

While still a student, he drew up, in collaboration with his fellow-students Eduardo Toda y Güell and José Ribera Sans, a project for the restoration of the monastery of Poblet.

Although Gaudí did not take too kindly to his academic studies, his years at the University broadened his historical knowledge and furthered his studies of science and technology. He also carried out scholarly research into architectural styles. He was already showing his tremendous versatility.

Before long he was invited to collaborate with some of the noted Catalan architects. Among these were Francisco del P. del Villar, with whom he is believed, though some doubt now exists, to have executed the *camarín* of the Virgin of Montserrat between 1876 and 1877; José Fontseré, with whom it is thought he might have worked on the park of the Cintedela in Barcelona–although doubt exists here too–between 1877 and 1882; Jose Serramalera, with whom he designed the illumination of the Muralla del Mar at Barcelona and the *Paseo Nacional* in the province of Barcelona; and Juan Martorell, with whom he designed the church of the convent of the Benedictines at Villaricos, at Gueva de Vera in 1882.

Some of the projects he carried out as a young man, among them the shop window for gloves, shown at the Paris International Exhibition in 1878, attracted the attention of Eusebio Güell who, throughout his life, was Gaudí's most important and faithful patron.

His youth was brilliant and worldly, and he took an active part in the cultural and social life of the city (he became a member of the Centre Excursionista, organised by the Catalan nationalists; he took an interest in social problems) and he was a frequent attender at the lively and cosmopolitan Güell salon. This contrasts strongly with the almost complete isolation and religious infatuation of his last years, in which he alienated himself absolutely from society with the result that in the end the only social relations he had were with the numerous visitors, students, and men-of-letters from all over the world who came to see his work, and whom he regaled at some length with discourses on 'Mediterranean architecture', his theories relating to mysticism and symbolism and his ideas on structural problems. This used to take place on the site of the Sagrada Familia, where towards the end of his life he installed himself in a small studio crammed with plans, funicular models, sketches and casts. He always spoke exclusively in Catalan. Schweitzer, who once went to see him at the Sagrada Familia, tells of how Gaudí, about to explain his mystical theory of the proportions imposed on the linear elements of the architecture to express symbols of the Trinity, said: 'This cannot be explained in French or in German or in English, so I will explain it to you in Catalan and you will understand it even if you don't understand the language'.

Gaudí had suffered from rheumatism from early childhood and adhered rigorously to the régime prescribed by Dr Kneipp, who imposed a vegetarian diet, homeopathic cures and long and regular walks. (From 1906 up till eight months before his death he lived in the Parc Güell and walked four and a half kilometres every day to the site of the Sagrada Familia; from there he would walk a further two kilometres to hear Mass at the church of San Filipo Neri, thus walking a total of about twelve kilometres a day.)

On 7th June, 1926, at about six in the evening, he was crossing a road on his way from the Sagrada Familia and San Filipo Neri and was knocked down by a tram. He was rescued but, as his clothing was very shabby, he was not recognised by anyone. He was taken to the Hospital for the Poor, where he died two days later without regaining consciousness.

59 Antoni Gaudí the year before his death

Chronological list of works

1869–70 Pupil at the Instituto Superiore of the Scolopi fathers at Reus, where he had worked for his *baccalauréat* since 1863. Collaborated with his schoolmates Eduardo Toda y Güell and José Ribera Sans in projecting the restoration of the monastery of Poblet. The manuscript of the project, which is some 60 pages long, is preserved in the library of the monastery, where it was deposited by Eduardo Toda when, some sixty years after its conception, he succeeded in reviving the proposal for the restoration. V. E. Casanelles, *Nuova Vision de Gaudí,* Barcelona, 1965. (Fig. 1 in R. Pane's book, *Antonio Gaudí,* Milan, 1964.)

1870 Went to Barcelona for the last year of his *baccalauréat.* Executed the following designs: candelabra; water reservoir; patio for a provincial government (picture by J. F. Ráfols, Barcelona, 1929); Spanish Pavilion for the Philadelphia Exhibition; monumental fountain for the Plaza de Cataluña (Fig. 6. J. F. Ráfols, Op. Cit.); Barcelona General Hospital; design for pier, competing for the school prize; monumental entrance to a cemetery (Fig. 7. J. F. Ráfols, Op. Cit.)

1876 Various designs for industrial machinery for the firm of Padros y Borras, in collaboration with the engineer, José Seramalera (Picture in R. Pane, Op. Cit.). Produced, probably during the course of this year, a poster for the Co-operative Mataronense.

1876–77 Collaborated with the architect Francisco de P. del Villar in building the *camarín* of the Virgin at Montserrat. This seems to be a contradiction of his most recent studies of Bohigas and Martinell. Moreover, his collaboration with the engineer José Fonseré on the works in the park of the Ciudadela of Barcelona does not seem to be in tune with his study of Martinell.

1878 Won the competition for the design of two lamps with six lights for the Plaza Real in Barcelona (Fig. 11); built his own desk (Fig. 2, J. F. Ráfols, Op. Cit.) and other furniture (chairs, stools, prayer stools) for the chapel of the Marquis of Comillás; designed a window for a glove-shop, which was sent to the Paris Universal Exhibition (design now in the Museum at Reus. Fig. 31, J. F. Ráfols, Op. Cit.); designed a flower-seller's kiosk at Comillás.

1878–80 Built Casa Vicens in Calle de las Carolinas, Barcelona. (Figs. 12–15, J. F. Ráfols, Op. Cit., and Plates 1–6).

1878–82 Designs for a factory, community centre and building complex for workers of La Obrera Matronense co-operative at Mataró near Barcelona. This was shown at the Paris Universal Exhibition of 1878 (Fig. 8, E. Casanelles, Op. Cit.); of these designs, he executed the roof of an industrial pavilion and a kiosk.

1879 Design for an allegorical cavalcade at Vallfogona de Rincorp; window of the Gilbert pharmacy at No. 4 Paseo de Gracia, now demolished.

1879–81. Altar, vestments and illumination for the Chapel of the College of Jesus and Mary at San André de Palomar, Barcelona, now largely destroyed.

1880 Collaborated with Serramalera on the illuminations for the Muralla del Mar (promenade) at Barcelona (designs for lamps: Fig. 5, J. F. Ráfols, Op. Cit.); street lighting for the Paseo Nacional in Barceloneta. Two lamps remain.

1880–81 Competition for the Casino at San Sebastian.

1880–81 Altar and pews for the Chapel of the College of Jesus and Mary at Tarragona, now destroyed.

1882 Designed the church of the Convent of the Benedictines of Villaricos, at Cuevas de Vera (Almería), under the guidance of the architect, Juan Martorell; designed a hunting lodge to be built at Garraf, near Barcelona, for Eusebio Güell (Fig. 29, J. F. Ráfols, Op. Cit.).

1883–87 Built the Finca Güell (Figs. 17–23, Plate 12) at Las Corts de Sarria, Barcelona; there remain the two factory blocks at the sides of the gate (the lodge is now a private house), a gateway in brick and ceramics, now much altered and restored (Fig. 23, J. F. Ráfols, Op. Cit.) and a brick stairway, now lost (Fig. 22, J. F. Ráfols, Op. Cit.).

1883 July. Designed an altar for a Neo-Gothic chapel at Alella, near Barcelona (Fig. 4). 3rd November. Took over responsibility for continuation of works on the crypt of the Sagrada Familia in Barcelona, begun in 1882 by Francisco de P. del Villar (Fig. 57, O. Bohigas, Op. Cit.).

1883–85 Built the villa El Capricho at Comillas (Santander) for Maximo Diaz de Quijano (Fig. 16, R. Pane, Op. Cit.).

1884 Designed a second altar for Tarragona, which was not completed; executed the altar of St Joseph in the crypt of the Sagrada Familia in Barcelona.

1885 Designed the furniture for his dining-room; designed and executed an altar for the Oratory of Casa Bocabella at No. 31 Calle Ausias March, Barcelona.

1885–89 Built the Palacio Güell at Nos. 3 and 5 Calle del Conde del Asalto, Barcelona (Figs. 24–28. Plates 7–11.).

1887–93 Plan for the restoration and reconstruction of the Archiepiscopal Palace at Astorga (Fig. 30–31).

1887 Designed and built the pavilion for the Naval Exhibition at Cadiz. November: received the commission, later revoked, to restore the interior decoration and floors of the Hall of One Hundred and main staircase of the Civic Palace of Barcelona.

1887–93 Built the walls of the apse of the Sagrada Familia.

1888 Was commissioned by the Marquis of Comillas to build a pavilion for the Compagnie Transatlantique at the Barcelona Universal Exhibition.

1889–94 Built the College of Santa Teresa of Jesus at No. 41 Calle de Granduxer, Barcelona (Plates 13–16).

1889 3rd March: started work on the restoration of the Archbishop's Palace at Astorga (Figs. 30–31).

1891–1903 Begun the Nativity façade of the Sagrada Familia and finished the crypt (Plates 37, 38).

1891 December: planned the building of Los Botines, Léon. (Fig. 32, R. Pane, Op. Cit.).

1892–93 Designed the home of the Franciscan Mission at Tangiers, to the commission of the Marquis of Comillas. This was never built (Fig. 10, J. F. Ráfols, Op. Cit.).

1892–94 Built Los Botines in the Plaza de San Marcel, Léon (Fig. 32).

1895 Designed the Güell family tomb at Montserrat.

1898 29th March. Handed over the designs for Casa Calvet, Barcelona. 24th December. Proposed revisions to this design, but they were not carried out.

1898–1904 Built Casa Calvet in Calle de Caspe, Barcelona (Fig. 33. Plates 17–22).

1898–1915 Built the crypt of the chapel of the Colonia Güell at Santa Coloma de Cervelló near Barcelona (Figs. 41–46).

1900 Designed a banner for the choral society of San Felice de Codines, near Barcelona. Designed a banner for the pilgrimage to the shrine of the Misericordia at Reus; made a preliminary study for the restoration of the exterior of the shrine.

1900–1914 Laid out and built the Parc Güell at the foot of the Muntaña Pelada, Barcelona (Figs. 37–39, Plates 26–35).

1900–2 Built the villa Bellesguard at Bonanova de Barcelona (Fig. 34, Plates 23–25).

1901–12 Built the boundary wall and gate of the Finca Miralles (Figs. 35, 36, R. Pane, Op. Cit.).

1901–2 Planned the restoration of the house of the Marquis of Casteldorsius in Calle de Mendizabal, Barcelona.

1903–26 Built the campaniles of the Nativity transept of the Sagrada Familia (Plates 39–40).

1904 Designed a stone bridge over the river Pomeret at Sarriá (Barcelona) which was not built: designed the group of sculptures for the first Glorious Mystery of the Rosary on the mountain of Montserrat; designed Casa Graner in Calle Nueva de Santa Eulalia, Barcelona. Only the foundations were laid, and have now disappeared; also for Luis Graner he built Casa Merçé, Barcelona, now demolished.

1904–14 Restored and remodelled the interior of the cathedral at Palma, Majorca (Fig. 40).

1905–7 Remodelled Casa Battló at 43 Paseo de Gracia, Barcelona (Figs. 47–50).

1905–10 Designed and built Casa Milá (la Pedrera) at No. 92 Paseo de Gracia, Barcelona (Figs. 51–53, Plate 36).

1908 Study for the restoration of the Gothic quarter of Barcelona.

1908–10 Designed the chapel of the Theresians at Barcelona.

1909 Built the school beside the Sagrada Familia (Figs. 54, 55).

1923 Produced designs for a chapel at the Colonia Calvet, for Torrelló.

1924 Designed a pulpit for Valencia.

1925–26 Built the campanile of San Bernabé above the Nativity façade of the Sagrada Familia.

Bibliography

MONOGRAPHS

Antoni Gaudí, *La seva vida. Les seves obres. La seva mort* (Miscellany), Barcelona, 1926; M. ROTGER CAMPLLONG, *Restauración de la catedral de Mallorca*, Palma di Majorca, 1907; AN DREU ESCUDER (J. TARRE), *L'arquitecte de la Sagrada Familia* (Miscelánea de la Editorial Poliglota), Barcelona, 1926; F. PUJOLS, *La vision artistica y religiosa d'En Gaudí*, Barcelona, 1927; J. F. RÁFOLS, *Antoni Gaudí*, 1852–1926; 1st Ed., Barcelona, 1928; 3rd Ed., Barcelona, 1952; 4th Ed., Barcelona, 1960; J. F. RÁFOLS–F. FOLGUERA, *Gaudí, el gran Arquitecto español*, Barcelona, 1928–29; J. PUIG BOADA, *El Temple de la Sagrada Familia*, Barcelona, 1929; J. MARAGALL, *En la Sagrada Familia; Obres completes de Johann Maragall* (Catalan series), vol. XV, Barcelona, 1933; J. MARAGALL, *El Templo que nace; Obras completas de Johann Maragall* (Catalan series), Barcelona, 1933; J. F. RÁFOLS, *Modernismo y Modernistes*, Barcelona, 1949; J. EDOUARD CIRLOT, *El Arte de Gaudí*, Barcelona, 1950; C. MARTINELL, *Gaudí y la Sagrada Familia comentada por ell mateix*, Barcelona, 1951; A. CIRICI PELLICER–J. GOMIS–J. PRATS VALLÉS, *La Sagrada Familia*, Barcelona, 1952; J. PUIG BOADA, *El Temple de la Sagrada Familia*, Barcelona, 1952; J. BERGÓS, *Gaudí, L'Home y l'Obra*, Barcelona, 1954; C. MARTINELL, *Gaudinismo*, Barcelona, 1954; C. MARTINELL, *Antoni Gaudí*, Milan, 1955; C. E. LE CORBUSIER–J. GOMIS–J. PRATS VALLÉS, *Gaudí*, Barcelona, February, 1958; E. CASANELLES, *Proyección universal del arte de Gaudí. Notas para una historia* (premio de los Juegos Florales del Casino de Terrasa), October, 1960; G. R. COLLINS, *Antoni Gaudí*, Milan, 1960; J. J. SWEENEY–J. L. SERT, *Antoni Gaudí*, Stuttgart, 1960; Milan, 1961; E. CASANELLES, *Maragall y el templo de la Sagrada Familia* (premio de los Juegos Florales), Barcelona, September, 1963; E. CASANELLES, *Nueva visión de Gaudí*, Barcelona, 1965; C. GIEDION-WELKER, *Parc Güell de Antonio Gaudí*; Barcelona, 1966; C. MARTINELL, *Antoni Gaudí*, Barcelona, 1967; J. PERUCHO–L. POMES, *Gaudí. Una arquitectura de anticipación*, Barcelona, 1967.

GENERAL WORKS

F. ROGENT Y PEDROSA–L. DOMENÉC Y MONTANER E ALTRI, *Arquitectura moderna de Barcelone*, Barcelona, 1897–1900; *Album d'Architecture moderne de Barcelone*, Barcelona, 1911; VICENTE LAMPÉRES Y ROMEA, *El Salón de Arquitectura* (Anuario de la Associación de Arquitectos de Catalunya), Barcelona, 1911; M. DIEULAFOY, *Art in Spain and Portugal*, New York, 1913; L. BREYER, *L'Art Chrétien, son développement iconographique des origines à nos jours*, Paris, 1918; J. E. BAYARD, *El Estilo Moderno*, Paris, 1919; *Antonio Gaudí y Cornet* (Enciclopedia universal ilustrada), vol. XXV, Barcelona, 1924; N. M. RUBIÓ Y TUDURÍ, *Diálegs sobre l'Arquitectura*, Barcelona, 1927; F. ELIAS, *L'escultura catalana moderna*, vol. II, Barcelona, 1928; KENJI IMAI, *Modern Architecture in Europe, Tokyo*, 1928; G. DESDEVISES DU DÉZERT, *Barcelone et les grands sanctua·res catalans*, Paris, 1930; C. MARTINELL, *L'Art catalá sota la unitat espanyola*, Barcelona, 1933; N PEVSNER, *Pioneers of the modern Movement from William Morris to Walter Gropius*, London, 1936; H. R. HOPE, *The Sources of Art Nouveau* (thesis for Harvard University), Cambridge, Mass. USA, 1943; A. CIRICI PELLICER, *Picasso antes de Picasso*, Barcelona, 1946; A. SARTORIS, *Gaudí* (in *Encyclopédie de l'Architecture nouvelle*), Milan, 1948–54; A. CALZADA, *Historia de la arquitectura española*, Barcelona, 1949; N. PEVSNER, *Pioneers of Modern Design from William Morris to Walter Gropius*, 2nd Ed., New York, 1949; A. CIRCI PELLICER, *El Arte Modernista Catalana*, Barcelona, 1951; J. F. RÁFOLS, *Gaudí* (in *Diccionario biográfico de artistas de Cataluña*), Barcelona, 1951–54; E. CIRLOT, *El estilo del siglo XX*, Barcelona, 1952; A. CIRICI PELLICER, *L'Arquitectura catalana*, Palma, Majorca, 1955; B. ZEVI, *Storia dell'Architectura moderna*, 3rd Ed., Turin, 1955; L. CUNHA, *Arquitectura religiosa moderna*, Oporto, 1957; H. RUSSELL-HITCHCOCK, *Architecture. Nineteenth and Twentieth Centuries*, Baltimore, 1958; J. VICENS I VIVES I MONTSERRAT LLORENS, *Industrials i politics (segle XIX)*, Barcelona, 1958; O BOHIGAS, *Un segle de vida catalana*, Barcelona, 1960, vol. II; F. and D. GETLEIM, *Christianity in Modern Art*, Milwaukee, 1961; J. VICENS I VIVES I MONTSERRAT LLORENS, *Un segle de vida catalana, 1814–1930*, Barcelona, 1961; E. CASANELLES, *Barcelona, la Ciudad, los Museos, la Vida*, Barcelona, 1962; J. CASSOU, LANGUI, N. PEVSNER, *Le origini dell'arte moderna*, Milan, 1962; 2nd ed., 1968; R. D'ABADAL E ALTRI, *Moments crucials de la historia de Catalunya*, Barcelona, 1962; R. SCHMUTZLER, *Art Nouveau–Jugendstil*, Stuttgart, 1962; E. JARDI, *Un altre Laocoont: Reflexións sobre els limits de les Arts Plàstiques*, Barcelona, 1963; P. VILLAR, *La Catalogne dans l'Espagne moderne*, Paris, 1963; E. GARRONI, *La crisi semantica delle arti figurative*, Rome, 1964; O. BOHIGAS, *Architettura modernista, Gaudí e il movimento catalano*, Turin, 1969.

SELECTION OF ARTICLES

W'R. LODIA, *Interior views from the House of Senor Güell, Barcelona, The Decorator and Furnisher*, New York, January, 1892; MIGUEL UTRILLO, *L'art en els edificis particulars, Pel y Ploma*, Barcelona, 1st July, 1900; BUENAVENTURA CONIL, *El Temple de la Sagrada Familia, Butlletí del Centre Excursionista de Catalunya*, Barcelona, April, 1901; F. ESCALAS, *Gaudí, Hispania*, Barcelona, 15th January, 1903; S. SELLES Y BARÓ, *El Parque Güell, Associación de Arquitectos de Cataluña*, Barcelona, 1903; B. FERRA, *Restauració de la Seu de Mallorca, Ilustració catalana*, Barcelona, August, 1905; F. CARDELLACH, *La mecanica d'En Gaudí, La Veu de Catalunya*, Barcelona, 20th January, 1906; J.F., *La Sagrada Familia, Ilustració catalana*, Barcelona, 18th May, 1906; J. MARAGALL, *Fora del Temps, Forma*, no. 16. vol. II, Barcelona, 1907; J. PIJOAN, *La obra de la Sagrada Familia, Forma*, no. 16, vol. II, Barcelona, 1907; A. SALVADOR CARRERAS, *Gaudí, (Impresión de viaje), Pequeñas monografías de Arte*, Madrid, November, 1907; C. MARQUINA, *La Sagrada Familia, L'Art et les Artistes*, vol. VI, 1908; S. SELLÉS Y BARÓ, *El Templo de la Sagrada Familia, Arquitectura y Construcción*, Barcelona, January, 1908; E. SORRA, *L'Architecture catalane contemporaine, L'Art décoratif*, X, 1908; E. JARDÌ, *Renaissance catalane; Architecture, L'Art public*, Brussels, December, 1909; H. BIDOU, *Les Salons de 1910, Gazette des Beaux-Arts*, VI, Paris, 1910; MARIUS ARY LEBLOND, *Gaudí et l'Architecture méditerranéenne, L'Art et les artistes*, XI, Paris, 1910; F. MIELERT, *Vom modernen Kirchenbau in Spanien, Archiv für Christliche Kunst*, XXVIII, Stuttgart, 1910; GLADIUS (R. RUCABADO), *Una casa viventa, Ciutat*, Tarrasa, April, 1910, U. TAVANTI, *Un architetto indipendente, Antonio Gaudí, Vita d'Arte*, V, Siena, 1910; A. BEARN, *Silhouettes catalanes: Antoni Gaudí, L'Action Jurassienne*, Dôle, 16th September, 1911; E. CHANOURDIE, *Una neuva arquitectura?, Arquietectura*, Buenos Aires, March/April, 1911; R. DE MAETZU, *El arquitecto del Naturalismo, Nuevo Mundo*, Madrid, March, 1911; J. MARTORELL, *Gaudí a Paris, Anuario de la Associación de Arquitectos de Cataluña*, Barcelona, 1911; M. STAKLEY, *The Story of the Creation told in stone in the great new Cathedral of Barcelona, The Craftsman*, New York, XXI, no. 5, 1912; M. VEGA Y MARCH, *El Templo de la Sagrada Familia, La Tribuna*, Barcelona. 28th October, 1912; J. MARIA DE DALMASSES BOCABELLA, *El Templo de la Sagrada Familia, El Correo Catalan*, Barcelona, 26th January, 1913; J. MARIA DE DALMASSES BOCABELLA, *Proyectomaqueta del Templo de la Sagrada Familia, El Propagador de la devoción a San José*, Barcelona, 15th November, 1913; (CIVIS), *La ciutades-jardines d'España, Barcelona: El Parque Güell, Civitas*, Barcelona, July, 1914; R. COLL Y PUJOL. *Para el Templo de la Sagrada Familia, Diario de Barcelona*, Barcelona. 19th March, 1914; J. SACS (FELIU ELIAS), *En Gaudí creador, Revista nova*, Barcelona, 23rd May, 1914; J. MARTÍ MATTLEU, *Impreciones a cerca del Templo de la Sagrada Familia, El Propagador de la devoción a San José*, Barcelona, April, 1914; A. MASRIERA, *Los arquitectos de entonces: siluetas de Isidro Reventós, Antonio Gaudí y Bonaventura Bassegoda, La Vanguardia*, Barcelona, 19th July, 1914; F. PUJOLS, *En Gaudí, Revista nova*, Barcelona, 23rd May, 1914; V. A. SALAVERRI, *Conversació con Gaudí, La Razón*, Montevideo, 1914; *La Actualidad*, Barcelona, 7th February, 1914: A. SALCEDO RUIZ, *El Palacio Episcopal de Astorga, El Universo*, Madrid, 21st June, 1914; F. CARDELLACH, *Los injeneros industriales el la Sagrada Familia, La Vanguardia*, Barcelona, 23rd February, 1915; J. DANÉS TORRAS, *El Templo de la Sagrada Familia, El Correo catalan*, Barcelona, 19th January, 1915; F. FOLGUERA, *La nova Catedral, La Veu de Catalunya*, Barcelona, 8th February, 1915; J. GARRIGA MASSÓ, *Una vision d'En Gaudí, Ilustració catalana*, Barcelona, 17th January, 1915; R. GHILONI, *El Templo Expiatorio de la Sagrada Familia, El Día gráfico*, Barcelona, 19th January, 1915; M. GONZÁLES ALBA, *Gaudí, La Cronica de Valls*, Valls, 30th January, 1915; R. JORI, *La Sagrada Familia, La Publicidad*, Barcelona. January, 1915; J. MARTÍ MATTLEU, *Las obras del Templo de la Sagrada Familia: en sayo de campanas: los campanarios, Diario de Barcelona*, Barcelona, 7th May, 1915: J. MARTÍ MATTLEU, *Monumentos españoles: El Templo de la Sagrada Familia, La Esfera*, Madrid, 10th April, 1915; M. (F. MATEU), *Per la Sagrada Familia. Ilustració catalana*, 17th January, 1915; J. MARATÓ Y GRAU, *La Catedral de Catalunya, Diario de Gerona*, Gerona, 3rd July, 1915; R. MUNTANER, *Pel temple de la Sagrada Familia, Vita Olotina*, Olot, 16th May, 1915; R. OLIVER, *La Catedral futura, La Academia Calasancia*, Barcelona, 10th February, 1915; E. PASQUAL D'AMIGÓ, *El Temple Expiatori de la Sagrada Familia, L'Apat, San Sadurní de Noya*, 17th April, 1915; J. PUIG BOADA, *Del Temple de la Sagrada Familia, La Veu Comarcal*, Ripoll, 3rd and 17th April and 1st May, 1915; J. PUIG BOADA, *Por el gran Templo Expiatorio, El noticiero universal*, Barcelona, January, 1915; F. PUJOL, *La Veu del Temple, Orfeon Catalan*, Barcelona, May, 1915; J. RUBIÓ, *Pro Sagrada Familia reacció, L'Apat, San Sadurní de Noya*, 13th June, 1915; A. RUIZ Y PABBO, *Por El Templo de la Sagrada Familia, La Vanguardia*, Barcelona, 7th February, 1915; J. STÜBBEN, *Stads Bauliches aus Barcelona, Zeitschrift für Bauwesen*, LXV, 1915, BUENAVENTURA BASSEGODA, *La Sagrada Familia, La Vanguardia*, Barcelona, 17th February, 1916; BUENAVENTURA BASSEGODA ED ALTRI, *El Temple de la Sagrada Familia, Anuario de la Associación de Arquitectos de Cataluña*, Barcelona, 1916; NARCISO MASÓ Y VALENTÍ, *Gaudí, genio de la Arquitectura, Diario de la Marina*, Havana, Cuba, 14th November, 1916: J. BORDAS, *Davant l'obra d'En Gaudí, La Cronica de Valls*, Valls, 7th April, 1917; J. MARIA DE DALMASSES BOCABELLA, *Explicación del grabado de la sección longitudinal del Templo de la Sagrada Familia, El Propagador de la devoción a San José*, 1st May, 1917; A. DE FOGUERALTA, *El Templo Canço, Patria*, Valls, 14th April, 1917; J. MARTÍ MATTLEU, *El Templo Expiatorio de la Sagrada Familia, El Universo*, Madrid, 8th April, 1917; C. MARTINELL, *El Templo de la Sagrada Familia, La Crónica de Valls*, Valls, 24th February, 1917; C. MARTINELL, *La Sagrada Familia, Temple de Catalunya, Patria*, Valls. 14th April, 1917; J. PARÉS, *Visita al Temple Expiatori de la Sagrada Familia, Butlletí del Centre Excursionista Barcelonès*, Barcelona, February, 1917: V. DE PEDRO. *La Arquitectura catalana, Caras y Caretas*, Buenos Aires: 1st October, 1917; J. POBLET, *Le Temple de l'expiació, Patria*, Valls, 14th April, 1917; D. SUGRAÑES, *La estabilidad en la construcción del Templo de la Sagrada Familia, Iberica*, VII, Madrid, March, 1917; D. SUGRAÑES, *La forma en el Templo de la Sagrada Familia, Iberica*, VII, Madrid, June, 1917; D. SUGRAÑES, *Visión de grandeza* (Lecture on 15th March, 1917), *El Propagador de la devoción a San José*, Barcelona, 15th April, 1917; J. MARIA DE DALMASSES BOCABELLA, *Explicación de las maquetas del Templo de la Sagrada Familia, El Propagador de la devoción a San José*, Barcelona, 1st April, 1918; J. LAGUIA LLITERAS, *La Basilica de la Sagrada Familia, Revista popular*, Barcelona, 14th April, 1918; J. M. LLOVERA, *A En Gaudí, Catalunya social*, Barcelona, 19th June, 1920; J. MARIA DE DALMASSES BOCABELLA, *Un jalón decisivo en el arte de construir, El Correo catalan*, Barcelona, 4th December, 1921; A. PLANA, *El Ferro i l'estil de l'arquitecte Gaudí, De l'Art de la Forja*, Barcelona, March, 1921; F. PUJOL, *L'obra del nostre Gaudí, De l'Art de la Forja*, Barcelona, March, 1921; F. PUJOL, *Representació universal del Gaudinisme* (collection of articles), *La Revista*, Barcelona, 1921; D. SUGRAÑES, *L'establitat en el Temple de la Sagrada Familia, La Veu de Catalunya*, Barcelona, 10th December, 1921; J. MARIA DE DALMASSES BOCABELLA, D. SUGRAÑES, *Estado de los trabajos del Templo de la Sagrada Familia, El Propagador de la devoción a San José*, Barcelona, 1st April, 1922; G. FORTEZA, *La restauració de la catedral de Mallorca, La ultima Hora*, Palma, 12th December,

1922; (T. GARCÉS), *L'arquitecte Gaudí. La Publicitat,* Barcelona, 10th June, 1922; J. MARTÍ MATTLEU, *El Templo expiatorio de la Sagrada Familia. El Correo catalan,* Barcelona, 23rd, 29th August, 10th, 17th, 24th September, 3rd, 8th, 17th, 22nd October, 1922; J. J. TALLMADGE, *The expiatory Temple of the Holy Family at Barcelona, Western Architecture,* XXXI, 1922; J. MARIA DE DALMASSES BOCABELLA, D. SUGRAÑES, *Los progresos de la construción de nuestro Templo, El Propagador de la devoción a San José,* Barcelona, 15th March, 1923; J. MARTÍ MATTLEU, *El Templo de la Sagrada Familia, Hormiga de Oro,* Special number, Barcelona, 17th March, 1923; D. SUGRAÑES, *Antoni Gaudí, Dant de l'arquitectura, Bella Terra,* Barcelona, Christmas/Epiphany, 1923–24; D. SUGRAÑES, *Disposició estatica del Temple de la Sagrada Familia, Annuario de los Arquitectos de Cataluña,* 1923; J. MARTÍ MATTLEU, *Impresiones a cerca del Templo de la Sagrada Familia, Diario de Barcelona,* 25th January to 15th May, 1924; R. BENET, *Gaudí, La Veu de Catalunya,* Barcelona, 18th December, 1925; M. ALUJAS. *L'eloqüéncia d'un temple, La Veu de Catalunya,* Barcelona, 6th July, 1926; A. BARCELÓ, *La Sagrada Familia, El Llamp,* Gandesa, 15th July, 1926; A. BARCELÓ, *Gaudí, La Veu de Catalunya,* 19th June, 1926; BUENAVENTURA BASSEGODA, *Antonio Gaudí, el Dante de la Arquitectura, La Vanguardia,* Barcelona, 23rd June, 1926; R. BENET, *La continuació de les obres de la Sagrada Familia, La Veu de Catalunya,* Barcelona, 28th August, 1926; R. BENET, *La lógica i la lirica d'Antonio Gaudí, La Veu de Catalunya,* Barcelona, 16th June, 1926; J. BERGÓS Y MASSÓ, *El cas Gaudí, Vida Lleidetana,* Lérida, 15th November, 1926; J. BERGÓS, *En Gaudí i la seva obra, La paraula cristiana,* Barcelona, July and September, 1926; L. BONET Y GARÍ, *En Gaudí, mestre, La Publicitat,* Barcelona, June, 1926, J. BIOSCA, *La continuació de les obres de la Sagrada Familia, La Veu de Catalunya,* Barcelona, 20th August, 1926; L. BONET Y GARÍ, *Les primeres obres del gran arquitecte Gaudí, Diari de Mataró,* Mataró, 12th June, 1926; J. BORDÁS (architect), *L'obra d'En Gaudí y la critica, L'Avi munné,* San Feliu de Guixols, 14th August, 1926; R. BRUGUERA, *La continuació de les obres de la Sagrada Familia, La Veu de Catalunya,* Barcelona, 18th August, 1926; B. S. F., *Gaudi, artista y catolico, Semanario Catolico de Reus,* Reus, 19th June, 1926; E. BUSQUETS CUNILL, *La continuació de les obres de la Sagrada Familia, La Veu de Catalunya,* Barcelona, 17th August, 1926; T. CAP DE VILA Y MIQUEL, *La continuació de les obres de la Sagrada Familia, La Veu de Catalunya,* Barcelona, 18th August, 1926; M. CAP DE VILA, *Un juicio de Puig y Cadafalch, El Debate,* Madrid, 13th June, 1926; J. CARNER, *Per la Sagrada Familia, La Veu de Catalunya,* Barcelona, 20th January, 1926; E. CASANOVAS, *La continuació de les obres de la Sagrada Familia, La Veu de Catalunya,* Barcelona, 13th August, 1926; H. CHAUVET, *El arquitecto Gaudí, El Correo catalan,* Barcelona, 20th June, 1926; H. COLLEYE, *L'art espagnol contemporain: Antoni Gaudí, La Métropole,* Anvers, 8th, 9th August, 1926; B. CONIL, *La continuació de les obres de la Sagrada Familia, La Veu de Catalunya,* Barcelona, 17th August, 1926; L. CREUS-VIDAL, *La continuació de les obres de la Sagrada Familia, La Veu de Catalunya,* Barcelona, 15th August, 1926; S. CUIXART Y PANELLA, *La continuació de les obres de la Sagrada Familia, La Veu de Catalunya,* Barcelona, 13th August, 1926; J. MARIA DE DALMASSES BOCABELLA, *Gaudí en el plan general del Temple Expiatoria de la Sagrada Familia, El Propagador de la devoción a San José,* Barcelona, 15th August, 1926; J. MARIA DE DALMASSES BOCABELLA, *La continuació de les obres de la Sagrada Familia, La Veu de Catalunya,* Barcelona, 28th August, 1926; R. DURAN CAMPS, *La continuació de les obres de la Sagrada Familia, La Veu de Catalunya,* Barcelona, 20th August, 1926; J. SACS (FELIU ELIAS), *Les Arts plastiques, Revista de Catalunya,* Barcelona, July, 1926; F. ELIAS, *La continuació de les obres de la Sagrada Familia, La Veu de Catalunya,* 13th August, 1926; A. ESCLASANS, *Gaudí mestre de Temples, El Dia,* Tarrasa, 17th June, 1926; F.J.O., *Antoni Gaudí, el Arquitecto genial, Revista de Oro,* Barcelona, June, 1926; F.J.O., *El Templo de la Sagrada Familia, poema mistico en piedra de Antonio Gaudi, Revista de Oro,* Barcelona, September, 1926; J. FOLCH I TORRES, *L'arquitecte Gaudí, Gaseta de les Arts,* Barcelona, III, July, 1926; F. FOLGUERA, *En Gaudí i les més modernes tendències arquitectoniques, Vida cristiana,* Barcelona, December, 1926; L. GIRONA Y CUYAS, *La continuació de les obres de la Sagrada Familia, La Veu de Catalunya,* Barcelona, 13th August, 1926; ANDRENIO (E. GOMEZ DE BAQUERIO), *Gaudí y el Renaccimiento catalano, La Vanguardia,* 15th June, 1926; J. MARIA JUNOI, *Antonio Gaudí, Bella Terra,* Barcelona, August, 1926; F. LABARTA, *La continuació de les obres de la Sagrada Familia, La Veu de Catalunya,* Barcelona, 20th August, 1926; A. LAMBERT, *Die Kirche Sagrada Familia in Barcelona, Deutsche Bauzeitung,* Berlin, LX, 15th May, 1926; A. DE LEMOS, *Gaudí el iluminado (Comentarios sobre su arte), Blanco y negro,* Madrid, 27th July, 1926; W. (MONS. PEDRO LISBONA), *Visualidades de Gaudí, El Correo catalan,* Barcelona, 20th June, 1926; J. LLADÓ CASANOVAS, *La continuació de les obres de la Sagrada Familia, La Veu de Catalunya,* 18th August, 1926; J. LLADÓ CASANOVAS, *La Sagrada Familia, La Publicitat,* Barcelona, 4th September, 1926; J. M. LÓPEZ PICÓ, *Antonio Gaudí, La Revista,* Barcelona, June, 1926; F. MANIC ILLA, *La continuació de les obres de la Sagrada Familia, La Veu de Catalunya,* 17th August, 1926; J. LLOGUERAS, *La continuació de les obres de la Sagrada Familia, La Veu de Catalunya,* 11th August, 1926; (J. MARTÍ MATTLEU), *El Temple de la Sagrada Familia, Aubada,* Barcelona, 6th March, 1926; A. MARTÍ MONTEYS, *La continuació de les obres de la Sagrada Familia, La Veu de Catalunya,* Barcelona, 13th August, 1926; C. MARTINELL, *Antoni Gaudí, Revista de Catalunya,* Barcelona, July, 1926; C. MARTINELL, *La originalitat d'En Gaudí, La Publicitat,* Barcelona, 13th June, 1926; F. MASPONS Y ANGLASELL, *Gaudí home de desordre, La Veu de Catalunya,* 15th June, 1926; L. MILLET, *Antoni Gaudí, Revista musical catalana,* Barcelona, July, 1926; M. DE MONTOLIN, *Hombres y cosas de Cataluna: Antonio Gaudí, La Prensa,* Buenos Aires, 8th August, 1926; OLEGUER DE MONTSERRAT, *En Gaudí i la seva obra, Catalunya social,* Barcelona, 19th June, 1926; V. OTTMANN, *Die Phantastische Stadt, Die Woche,* Berlin, 28th August, 1926; J. PUIG BOADA, *L'architecte Gaudí, Revue internationnelle de la proprieté foncière bâtie,* Paris, September, 1926; F. POJOL, *La continuació de les obres de la Sagrada Familia, La Veu de Catalunya,* Barcelona, 28th August, 1926; ROQUE GUINART (L. RIBER), *El Arquitecto Antoni Gaudí, El Sol,* Madrid, 12th June, 1926; R. CAMPFULLÓS (L. RIBER), *Gaudí constructor de catedrales, Diario de Barcelona,* 11th July, 1926; E. ROCA, *La continuació de les obres de la Sagrada Familia, La Veu de Catalunya,* Barcelona, 18th August, 1926; N. M. RUBIÓ Y TUDURI, *El Parque Güell, espacio libre de la ciudad, Barcelona Atracción,* Barcelona, August, 1926; R. RUCABADO, *Consideración sobre Gaudí, Diario de Sabadell,* Sabadell, 3rd July, 1926; R. RUCABADO, *En Gaudí a Santa Creu, La Veu de Catalunya,* Barcelona, 13th June, 1926; S. SEDO, *L'obra magna de Gaudí, Diario de Reus,* Reus, 15th and 18th June, 1926; D. SUGRAÑES, *Gaudí, l'architecte de la Sagrada Familia, Revista del Centre de Lectura,* Reus, 1st and 15th August, 1926; P. SURRIBAS ALSINA, *La continuació de les obres de la Sagrada Familia, La Veu de Catalunya,* Barcelona, 17th August, 1926; 'MARCIAL' (TRICCA ROSTOLL) *El poeta de la pedra, Diario do Mataró,* Mataró, 14th June, 1926; J. VALLÉS Y PUJOLS, *Un hombro prodigio y un monumento prodigioso, La Nación,* Buenos Aires, 18th August, 1926; M. VEGA Y MARCH, *Antoni Gaudí, La Vanguardia,* Barcelona, 19th June, 1926; M. ALAYO, *L'exposició Gaudí, Gaseta de Vilafranca, Vilafranca del Panadés,* 2nd June, 1927; R. BENET, *Exposició Gaudí, La Veu de Catalunya,* Barcelona, 24th June, 1927; R. BENET, *Gòtic Catala, La Veu de Catalunya,* Barcelona, 3rd June, 1927; L. BONET (Architect), *L'obra arquitectionica d'En Gaudí, La Ciutat y la Casa,* Barcelona, VI, 1927; L. BONET Y GARÍ, *El arquitecto Don Antonio Gaudí, El Propagador de la devoción a San José,* Barcelona, 1st June, 1927; J. MARIA DE DALMASSES BOCCABELLA, *D. Antoni Gaudí y Cornet, Associación espiritual de devotes de San José* (1926), Josephine Calendar for 1927; 'FRIEND', *La pedrera, Mediterraneo,* Barcelona, 2nd April, 1927; A. LAMBERT, *Église expiatoire de la Sainte Famille à Barcelone par Antoni Gaudí, La Construction Moderne,* Paris, X, July, 1927; C. MARTINELL, *El mestratge intim de Gaudí, El Propagador de la devoción a San José,* Barcelona, June, 1927; M. MUNTADAS ROVIRA, *La obra genial de Gaudí, Mediterraneo,* Barcelona, 2nd April, 1927; F. DE P. QUINTANA, *Les formes guerxes del temple de la Sagrada Familia, La Ciutat i la Casa,* VI, Barcelona, 1927; C. RAHOLA, *Un aspecte de Gaudí, La Publicitat,* Barcelona, 24th June, 1927; 'H. DE RIBAGORZA' (VERDAGUER), *Gaudí, Hoja oficial de la Provincia de Barcelona,* Barcelona, 20th June, 1927; L. RIBER, *Antoni Gaudí el constructor de la Sagrada Familia, Mundo ibérico,* Barcelona, 5th July, 1927; A. SALVADOR CARRERAS, *Un recuerdo de Gaudí, Arquitectura,* IX, no. 93, Madrid, 1927; P. M. STRATTON, *The Sagrada Familia church, The Builder,* CXXXIII, London, August, 1927; D. SUGRAÑES, *D. Antonio Gaudí y Cornet, Associación de Arquitectos de Cataluña,* MCMXXVII, Barcelona; R. VAYREDA, *La qualitat en l'obrade N' Antonio Gaudí, D'aci i d'allá,* Barcelona, January, 1927; M. ALCOVER, *La seo de Mallorca y su restauración por D. Antonio Gaudí, La Razón y Fé,* Madrid, 10th and 25th June, 1928; R. ARTIGAS, *Gaudí creador d'estructures, La Veu de Catalunya,* Barcelona, 11th June, 1928; R. BENET, *El gust de Gaudí, La Veu de Catalunya,* Barcelona, 11th June, 1928; A. BUIL, *Els ferros d'En Gaudí, La Veu de Catalunya,* Barcelona, 11th June, 1928; F. FOLGUERA, *Arquitectura moderna, Il Anuari dels Amics de l'Art litúrgic,* Barcelona, 1928; G. FORTEZA, *En Gaudí, Almanac de les Lletres,* Mallorca, 1928; M. GIFREDA, *Le Corbusier a Barcelona, La Publicitat,* Barcelona, 18th May, 1928; J. PUIG BOADA, *Antoni Gaudí, Il Anuari dels Amics de l'Art litúrgic,* Barcelona, 1928; J. F. RÁFOLS, *Gaudí, fragmentos de una biografía, Arquitectura,* X, Barcelona, 1928; VILA SAN JUAN, *Barcelona. La filosofía del Templo y su arte, La Esfera,* Madrid, 14th January, 1928; E. VAUGH, *Gaudí, Architectural Review,* LXVII, London, June, 1930; J. F. RÁFOLS, *Gaudí, Enciclopedia italiana di Scienze, Lettere e Arti,* XVI, Milan, 1932, J. CASSOU, *Gaudí, Formes,* XXXII, Paris, 1933; S. DALÍ, *De la beauté terrifiante et comestible de l'architecture Modern-Style, Minotaure,* III–IV, Paris, 1933; D. SUGRAÑES, *Gaudí y l'urbanisme, El Matí,* Barcelona, 31st July 1932; L. BONET, *Museo de peregrinaciones. Se instalará en el Palacio de Gaudí, El Pensamiento Astorgano,* 2nd April, 1936; KENYI IMAI, *Architecture of Barcelona: Sagrada Familia, Kentiku Sekai,* VIII, Tokyo, August, 1939; N. TESCH, *Antoni Gaudí, Byggmästaren,* X, Stockholm, 1948; G. M. SOSTRES MALUQUER, *Sentimiento y Simbolismo del espacio, Projectos y Materiales,* New York, September/October, 1949; E. CIRLOT, *El arte de Gaudí, Spazio,* 1, Milan, August, 1950: G. E. KIDDER SMITH, *Report from Spain and Portugal, Architectural Forum,* XLII, New York, 1950: P. LINDER, *Encuentros con Antoni Gaudí, Mar del Sur,* II, Lima, March/April, 1950; R. OPISSO, *Recuerdo de Gaudí, Diario de Barcelona,* 1950; G. M. SOSTRES MALUQUER, *El Funcionalismo y la nueva plastica, Boletín de información de la dirección jeneral de Arquitectura,* IV, Madrid, July, 1950; B. ZEVI, *Un genio catalona, Metron,* 38, Rome, September/October, 1950; R. OPISSO, *Recuerdo de Gaudí, Diario de Barcelona,* Barcelona, 1951; C. FERRATER, *Gaudí en el Museo municipal de Reus, Reus,* Reus, 28th June, 1952; F.L.P. (FLOUQUET), *Surréalisme et Architecture: À propos de Gaudí y Cornet, La Maison,* VIII, Paris, November, 1952; R. OPISSO, *Recuerdo de Gaudí, Diario de Barcelona,* Barcelona, 1952; N. PEVSNER, *The Strange Architecture of Antoni Gaudí, The Listener,* XLVII, London, 7th August, 1952; F. DE P. QUINTANA, *Gaudí* (lecture), *Templo,* LXXXVII, Barcelona, August, 1952; A. SARTORIS, *Gaudí poliforme, Numero,* III, Florence, December, 1952; O. JIMENO, *Antoni Gaudí y la originalidad arquitectónica, El arquitecto peruano,* Lima, July/August, 1953: R. OPOSSO, *Recuerdo de Gaudí, Diario de Barcelona,* Barcelona, 1953; R. SCHOELKOPF, *Antoni Gaudí, architect, Perspecta,* New Haven, II, 1953; J. J. SWEENEY, *Antoni Gaudí, Magazine of Art,* New York, XLVI, May, 1953; INO YULCH AND OTHERS, *The Sacred Family church, World's contemporary architecture,* IX, 1953; A. MORAVIA, *Gaudí, Corriere della sera,* Milan, 6th May, 1954; J. L. SERT, *Introduzione a Gaudí, Casabella,* Milan, 212, August/September, 1954; S. GIEDION WELKER, *Bildafte Kachel-Compositionen von Antoni Gaudí, Werk,* XLII, Zurich, April, 1955, J. GRADY, *Nature and the Art Nouveau, Art Bulletin,* XXXVII, London, 1955, B. PETTERSON, *Antoni Gaudí ett Ornamentikens geni, Sydsvenska dagbladet,* Malmö, 27th February, 1955: J. L. SERT, *Gaudí, visionnaire et précurseur, L'Œil,* II, Paris, February, 1955; L.Z. (ZAHN), *Antoni Gaudí und seine Kathedrale, Das Kunstwerk,* IX, Baden-Baden, 5, 1955–56; O. BOHIGAS, *La Arquitectura catalana moderna en seis fechas, Revista,* Barcelona, 8th May, 1956; A. CASSI RAMELLI, *Mestiere e maestria de Antoni Gaudí, Architectura-Cantiere,* Milan, II, December, 1956; R. OPISSO, *Recuerdo de Gaudí, Diario de Barcelona,* Barcelona, 1956; J. J. SWEENEY, *Is yesterday's fantasy tomorrow's working geometry?, Architectural Forum,* New York, CIV, March, 1956; A. ALBANESI, *Divagazioni su Antonio Gaudí: un tempio come vaso spaziale, architetto Enrico Costiglioni, L'Architettura,* September, 1957; D. ASHTON, *Antoni Gaudí, Kraft Horizons,* XVII, New York, November/December, 1957;

M. DE LUIGI, *Un pittore giudica l'architettura; Antoni Gaudí, L' Architettura*, III, Roma, 22nd August, 1957; F. L. P. DEWALD, *Antoni Gaudí, Spaans Architect, Bouwkunding wéekblad*, Amsterdam, LXXV, 19th March, 1957; A. KERRIGAN, *Gaudinianism in Catalonia, Arts*, New York, XXXII, December, 1957; J. F. RÁFOLS, *Valoración de Gaudí por los de Pel y Ploma, Destino*, Barcelona, December, 1957; M. BRUNATI E ALTRI, *Eredità dell'800: spazio e sintesi plastica nel genio di Barcelona, L'Architettura*, Rome, IV, May, 1958; A. HENZE, *Antonio Gaudís Sühnetempel der Heiligen Familie, Festshrift Martin Wackernagel*, Böhlau, Colonia, 1958; F. HERMAN, *Inimitable Gaudí, Progressive Architecture*, XXXIX, 1958; H. R. HITCHCOCK, *The work of Antoni Gaudí y Cornet, Architectural association journal*, London, LXXIV, November, 1958; E. HOFFMANN, *Current and Forthcoming Exhibitions* (Gaudí exhibition in New York), *Burlington Magazine*, C, 1958; C. L. RAGGHIANTI, *Antoni Gaudí, Sele Arte*, 35, Florence, March/April, 1958; J. TYRWHITT, *Gaudí Symposium at the Museum of Modern Art, Architectural Review*, New York, CXXIII, 1958; U. CONRAD–H. G. SPERLICH, *Phantastische Architektur, Zodiac*, Milan, 5, 1959; D. EDQUIST, *Arkitektur och Daskap, Arkitektur*, XXXVIII, 1959; R. ESVEGARD, *En Katalansk Konstnäi, Konstrevy*, Stockholm, 5/6, 1959; A. FORMER, *Gaudí, arkiturens okände mästare, Byggands Ingenjören*, Stockholm, 3, 1959; L. KROLL, *Sur l'architecture de Gaudí, La Maison*, Brussels, IX, September, 1959; L. SERT, *A pictorial excursion into the unique Gaudí world, Progressive Architecture*, XL, New York, 1959; P. E. SKRIVER, *Gaudí, Arkitekten*, Copenhagen, 18th September, 1959; O. BOHIGAS, *Problemas en la continuació de la Sagrada Familia, Gaudí; Centro de Estudios Gaudinistas*, Barcelona, 1960; E. CASANELLES, *El Parque Güell, Barcelona, ciutad de Gaudí, Destino*, Barcelona, 24th December, 1960; J. JOEDICKE, *Willkür und Bindung im Werk von Antonio Gaudí, Bauen-Wohnen*, Zurich, May, 1960; N. PEVSNER, *Gaudí–Pioneer or Outsider, Architects Journal*, London, December, 1960; E. RODITI, *Le nez en l'air à Barcelone, Les Parisiens*, Paris, December, 1960; B. ZEVI, *L'incompreso di Barcelona, L'Espresso*, 28th August, 1960; E. CASANELLES, *El cinquentenario de la Pedrera. Carta a un estudiante americano, Destino*, Barcelona, 18th March, 1961; E. CASANELLES, *Gaudí en Mallorca, Destino*, Barcelona, 23rd December, 1961; F. CERES, *Antoni Gaudí, arquiteto do 'Art Nouveau', Leitura*, Rio de Janeiro, 45, 1961; P. DU COLOMBIER, *Revanche de Gaudí, La Revue Française*, Paris, May, 1961; J. GALLEGO, *Las fuentes del siglo XX, Apoteosis de Gaudí, Crónica de Paris, Goya*, Madrid, 40, 1961; K. A. GOETZ, *Gaudis Beitrag zur Sakralarchitektur, Kunstkalender für das Jahr 1962*, Heidelberg, 1961; K. A. GOETZ, *Predigt aus Stein? Grösse und Tragik des Antonio Gaudí, Merian*, Hamburg, 1961; JOSHIRO IKEHARA, *Construction of Gaudí's Architecture, Kindai Kentiku*, Tokyo, XV, no. 3, March, 1961; YUITIRO KOJIRO, *Two directions in future; Antonio Gaudí and Antonio Sant'Elia, Kindai Kentiku*, Tokyo, XV, no. 3, March 1961; D. MACKAY, *Tres scriptores estrangers encarants amb Gaudí, Serra d'Or*, Monasterio de Montserrat, 3, March, 1961; C. RODRIGUEZ AGUILERA, *Gaudí artista moderno, Gran Via*, Barcelona, 6th May, 1961; YOSIAKI TONO, *Architecture of Antonio Gaudí, Kindai Kentiku*, Tokyo, XV, no. 3, March, 1961; J. REZNIK, *Gaudí, o precursor, Crítica de Arte*, Rio de Janeiro, no. 1, 1961–62; E. CASANELLES, *Gaudí ante Monserrat, Destino*, Barcelona, 26th May, 1962; J. DE CASTRO ARINES, *Gaudí y su mundo, Informaciones*, Madrid, 30th October, 1962; A. HENZE, *Eine Kirche des 19 Jahrhunderts Antonio Gaudí, Sühnetempel der Heiligen Familie in Barcelona, STZ*, 37, Berne, September, 1962; J. JOEDICKE, *Antonio Gaudí, L'Architecture d'aujourd'hui*, Paris, 102, June/July 1962; A. LLOPIS, *Vallfogono y un dibujo inédito de Gaudí, Destino*, Barcelona, 13th January, 1962; M. RAGON, *Antonio Gaudí, précurseur de l'actuelle architecture baroque, Jardin des Arts*, Paris, 89, 1962; L. BONET, *La Entidad Amigos de Gaudí comble diez anos, Solidaridad Nacional*, Barcelona, 16th March, 1963, E. CASANELLES, *Gaudí en el Japon, Destino*, Barcelona, 29th June, 1963; J. M. GARRUT, *Gaudí, capital Barcelona, Diario de Barcelona*, Barcelona, 21st July, 1963; M. MARNAT, *Née au siècle d'or des lumières, l'architecture contemporaine réconcilie le réalisme et le phantastique, Combat*, Paris, 30th December, 1963; S. J. GONZALES MOLINA, *El arte de Gaudí triumfa en el Japon, La Vanguardia Española*, Barcelona, 7th July, 1963; J. PEDRO POSANI, *Don Antonio Gaudí, arquitecto genial creador de formas, Boletin Informativo de la Universidad Centrale de Venezuela*, Caracas, 15th June, 1963; 'SEMPRONIO', *Gaudí, Japan (Las casas como son), Diario de Barcelona*, Barcelona, 28th June, 1963; HIROSHI TESHIGAWARA, *Gaudí in Japan, Interior Design*, Tokyo, no. 3, June, 1963; L. PAUWELS, *Antoni Gaudí, Pianeta*, Florence, I, 1964; O. BOHIGAS, *Notes sobre Gaudí i la Sagrada Familia, Serra d'Or*, Montserrat, April, 1965; V. GIRARDI, *Alla ricerca di Antoni Gaudí, L'Architettura*, XIV, no. 159, January, Rome, 1969.

OTHER ARTICLES FROM REVIEWS AND PERIODICALS

A modern house at Barcelona, American Architect and Building News, Boston, July, 1892; *La Caso Battló al Passeig de Gràcia, Illustració catalana*, Barcelona, 10th March, 1907, and 19th June, 1910; *Gaudí, Ilustracio catalana*, 19th June, 1910; *Il tempio espiatorio della Sacra Famiglia, L'Osservatore Romano*, Rome, 18th December, 1922 and 6th January, 1923; *El Templo Expiatorio de la Sagrada Familia creará una escuela y harà época, El Siglo Futuro*, Madrid, 8th January, 1923; *Gaudí, Revue politique et littéraire, Revue bleue*, Paris, 15th August, 1925; *Gaudí, Condal*, Barcelona, June, 1926; *Cuadernos de arquitectura*, Barcelona, XXVI, April/June, 1956 (Number devoted to Gaudí); *Antoni Gaudí Cornet, La Gralla, Granollers*, 13th June, 1926; *De Verdaguer a Gaudí, La Veu de Catalunya*, Barcelona, 11th June, 1927; *El arquitecto Gaudí, Patria*, Palma de Mallorca, 4th April, 1928; *Recensione al volume di Ráfols e Folguera, Byggmästaren*, X, 1929 21 articles on Gaudí in *El Matí*, Barcelona, 21st June, 1936; *Gaudí centenary competition* (notes on the competition held to celebrate the birth of Gaudí), *Architectural Review*, New York, CXII, 672, December, 1952; 11 Articles on Gaudí in *Cupola*, Barcelona, no. 319, 1952; *Fantastic Catalan, Time*, London, 3, LIX, no. 4, 28th January, 1952; *Gaudí, Werk*, XXXIX, no. 12, December, 1952; *Gaudí, Revista nacional de Arquitectura*, Madrid, XIII, July, 1953; Reviews of *El arte de Gaudí* by Cirlot, *La Sagrada Familia de A. Gaudí* by Cirici Pellicer, *El templo de la Sagrada Familia, sintesis de arte* by Puig Boada in *Architectural Record*, CXVI, July, 1954; *Packet of photographs from C*

Cataluña: in the attics of Gaudí's Casa Milá, Interiors, CXV, 7th February, 1956; *Antonio Gaudí, nuove visioni della casa Milá a Barcellona, L'Architettura*, Rome, II, 9th July, 1956; *Gaudí, Chiesa e Quartiere*, Bologna, V, March, 1958; (Report on the Gaudí exhibition in New York and on a private exhibition in Milan held by Mario Brunato, Sandro Mendini, Ferruccio Villa, *Domus*, Milan, CCCXLII, May, 1958; *Fantastic Architecture in a stern setting* (Note on the Gaudí exhibition at the Museum of Modern Art in New York) in *Interiors*, New York, CXVII, 8th March, 1958; *Papeles de Son armadas* (number devoted to Gaudí, essays by Casanelles, Azorin, Sartoris, Palencia, Wenterdahl, Aranguren, Chueca Goitia, Buero Valleyo, Kerrigan, Zabaleta, Popovici, De la Serna).

Exhibitions

EXHIBITIONS OF GAUDÍ'S WORK

Musée d'Art Moderne, Paris, 1910, *Gaudí*. Barcelona, 1927, *Gaudí*. Studio Mendini, Villa Brunati, Milan, 1958 (catalogue contains article by Sandro Mendini: *Gaudí, a precursor*). Museum of Modern Art, New York, 18th December, 1957–23rd February, 1958 (preface to catalogue by Arthur Drexler and Henry-Russell Hitchcock: *Gaudí*). Buenos Aires, 1960 (Catalogue contains article by Antonio Bonet: *Antoni Gaudí*). Museum für Kunst, Baden-Baden, 1961 (Presented by Wilhelm Boeck: *Antonio Gaudí*). Centro italiano di informazione e di divulgazione, Genoa, September/October, 1961 (presented by Giuliano Forno: *Gaudí*).

EXHIBITIONS INCLUDING GAUDÍ'S WORK

Museum of Modern Art, New York, *Fantastic Art, Dada, Surrealism* (presented by Alfred Barr Jr.). Kunstgewerbemesuem, Zurich, 1952 *Um 1900. Art Nouveau und Jugendstil*. Museum of Modern Art, New York, 1958: *Art Nouveau. Art and Design at the turn of the century*. Musée d'Art Moderne, Paris, 1960–61: *Les sources du XXe siècle. Les Arts en Europe de 1884 à 1914*. (Presented by Pevsner, Cassou, Langui). Gemeente Museum, The Hague, 1960–61: *Nieuwe Kunst Rend 1900*. Ostend Museum, 1968: *Europa 1900*.